D1025874

Partnering in the Learning Marketspace

Ann Hill Duin
Linda L. Baer
Doreen Starke-Meyerring

Partnering in the Learning Marketspace

EDUCAUSE

Leadership Strategies No. 4

JOSSEY-BASS
A Wiley Company
San Francisco

This book is part of the Jossey-Bass Higher and Adult Education Series.

 Manufactured in the United States of America on Lyons Falls Turin Book.
This paper is acid-free and 100 percent totally chlorine-free.

Library of Congress Cataloging-in-Publication Data

Duin, Ann Hill.
  Partnering in the learning marketspace / Ann Hill Duin, Linda L.
Baer, Doreen Starke-Meyerring.
    p. cm.—(EDUCAUSE leadership strategies; no. 4)
Includes bibliographical references (p.) and index.
  ISBN 0-7879-5012-2
  1. Education, Higher—Computer network resources. 2. Internet
in education. 3. Mentoring in education. 4. University
cooperation. I. Baer, Linda L. date– II. Starke-Meyerring,
Doreen, date– III. Title. IV. Series.
  LB1044.87.D86 2001
  004.6—dc21

00-012950

FIRST EDITION
PB Printing 10 9 8 7 6 5 4 3 2 1

The EDUCAUSE Leadership Strategies series addresses critical themes related to information technology that will shape higher education in the years to come. The series is intended to make a significant contribution to the knowledge academic leaders can draw upon to chart a course for their institutions into a technology-based future. Books in the series offer practical advice and guidelines to help campus leaders develop action plans to further that end. The series is developed by EDUCAUSE and published by Jossey-Bass. The sponsorship of PricewaterhouseCoopers LLP makes it possible for EDUCAUSE to distribute complimentary copies of books in the series to more than 1,700 EDUCAUSE member institutions, organizations, and corporations.

EDUCAUSE is an international nonprofit association with offices in Boulder, Colorado, and Washington, D.C. The association is dedicated to helping shape and enable transformational change in higher education through the introduction, use, and management of information resources and technologies in teaching, learning, scholarship, research, and institutional management. EDUCAUSE activities include an educational program of conferences, workshops, seminars, and institutes; a variety of print and online publications; strategic/policy initiatives such as the National Learning Infrastructure Initiative, the Net@EDU program, and the Center for Applied Research; and extensive Web-based information services.

EDUCAUSE

- provides professional development opportunities for those involved with planning for, managing, and using information technologies in colleges and universities
- seeks to influence policy by working with leaders in the education, corporate, and government sectors who have a stake in the transformation of higher education through information technologies
- enables the transfer of leading-edge approaches to information technology management and use that are developed and shared through EDUCAUSE policy and strategy initiatives
- provides a forum for dialogue between information resources professionals and campus leaders at all levels
- keeps members informed about information technology innovations, strategies, and practices that may affect their campuses, identifying and researching the most pressing issues

Current EDUCAUSE membership includes more than 1,700 campuses, organizations, and corporations. For up-to-date information about EDUCAUSE programs, initiatives, and services, visit the association's Web site at www.educause.edu, send e-mail to info@educause.edu, or call 303-449-4430.

PRICEWATERHOUSE COOPERS

PricewaterhouseCoopers is a leading provider of professional services to institutions of higher education, serving a full range of educational institutions—from small colleges to large public and private universities to educational companies.

PricewaterhouseCoopers (www.pwcglobal.com) is the world's largest professional services organization, drawing on the knowledge and skills of more than 150,000 people in 150 countries to help clients solve complex business problems and measurably enhance their ability to build value, manage risk, and improve performance in an Internet-enabled world.

PricewaterhouseCoopers refers to the member firms of the worldwide PricewaterhouseCoopers organization.

Contents

Foreword

The idea of a market where teachers and learners can trade is not new. It is the medium in which it takes place that is new and warrants changing the term *marketplace* to *marketspace*.

A market is a space where people gather to trade and communicate. We have recognized for more than a decade that the market being created by the new generation of telecommunications is essentially commercial in nature and the Internet is enabling a global trade in teaching (Tiffin, 1990). The idea expressed in *Partnering in the Learning Marketspace*—of a marketplace in learning—emphasizes the dynamic partnership that is involved in the learning process.

Education is a communication process whereby people in the role of teachers help people in the role of learners to apply knowledge to problems. Whether the teachers are called facilitators or tutors, whether the learners are students or customers, whether knowledge is known as skill or competency, and whether problems are considered applications or tasks, the simple fact is that these are the critical interacting components in the transaction called education. If learners do not need teachers, and if knowledge has no application, then there is no need for education.

It is possible to envision this communication process in terms of a market. Learners can be seen as customers seeking to learn how to apply knowledge to the problems of life, just as they may buy food to deal with their hunger. Teachers can be seen as sellers not of knowledge itself but of a service. They teach people to apply knowledge.

Education can take place in the home or as part of learning to do a job, but it is the kind of education that takes place in a classroom that has the potential to be commercial. Someone has to pay for the teachers, the books, the buildings, and the transport systems that bring the teachers and students together. Primarily, whereas education has traditionally been for the young, it is parents who pay. But in the case of private education, the parent pays directly and a market exists, whereas in public education the parent pays through taxes and there is no market.

Over the last century and a half, with the rise of industrial society, nation-states have taken control of education. The whole pyramidal paraphernalia of national education systems has been dedicated to preparing people to be good citizens. They learn to read and write in the national language; to trade in a national currency; to sing the national songs; to pray to the national god; to take pride in the national history, geography, art, and literature; and to accept the national law. Essentially, it was state legislatures that defined who was allowed to teach, what constituted the curriculum, and the process whereby degrees and certificates were awarded. Education became a public good, a citizen's right, and a compulsory rite of passage.

Of course, with the exception of some of the communist and socialist countries, private education continued through the period of industrial society. Even if only on the level of private lessons after school, there has always been a market for teachers to sell their skills directly to learners or their parents. In countries such as the United States, with strong concern for capitalist principles and lifelong learning, market-based education for which the user pays has played a strong part in the national education system. However, such markets for teaching have existed within the confines of the boundaries of nation-states and have had to conform to their laws.

All this began to change in the last decade of the twentieth century, with the coming of the Internet. Suddenly learning, like television and trade, has been freed from national boundaries. It has become part of the process of globalization. It is now possible for anyone anywhere to get an education on the Internet, provided of course that he or she can pay. Global education on the Internet is not supported through taxes. So the market in education is back, only this time it is a global market. For the moment, the market is essentially at the tertiary level of education, where education is voluntary, but this will not last. Already schoolchildren, "school leavers," and adults at every level are seeking for themselves on the Internet what they want in an education.

In 1995, we published *In Search of the Virtual Class: Education in an Information Society*. Two years later, on the basis of the book and in conjunction with an international group of academics who shared our interests, we formed the Global Virtual University (GVU). So far, this has been an academic project focused on the nature of the university in an information society and the need for a paradigm shift. But it is now attracting commercial interest. In terms of a learning marketspace, it favors Lalita Rajasingham's academic agora model, harking back to the Greek marketplace as a center of civic as well as commercial life, and seeks to be an equal mixture of commercial forces and imperatives for the public good (in a global sense). Is it possible to have a dynamic tension between the two that is creative? Can there be a learning marketspace where commercial undertaking cannot be at the expense of academic values, nor academic initiatives be without a sound commercial basis? Will this be possible in the regulatory apparatus that the World Trade Organization is devising for information services such as education?

The ideas and issues raised in *Partnering in the Learning Marketspace* reflect a global struggle to understand the nature of tertiary education in an information society. We are in a time of competing paradigms, and this is reflected in competing metaphors. Dennis

Gooler (1986) saw networked learning as a public utility; Parker Rossman (1992) wrote of an emerging worldwide electronic university; we seek a global virtual university. Terms such as *cyberuni* and *cyberlearning*, *network college* and *netlearning*, and *e-university* and *e-learning* proliferate. This book introduces a new paradigm. Which of these versions of the educational environment of the future will our children accept as what Thomas Kuhn (1962) called the norm paradigm?

Watch this marketspace to find out.

JOHN TIFFIN
Professor Emeritus of Communications
    Studies and Chancellor
Global Virtual University

LALITA RAJASINGHAM
Senior Lecturer, School of
    Communication and Information
    Management
Victoria University of Wellington,
    New Zealand

References

Gooler, D. D. *The Educational Utility: The Power to Revitalize Education and Society.* Englewood Cliffs, N.J.: Educational Technology Publications, 1986.

Kuhn, T. S. *The Structure of Scientific Revolutions.* Chicago: University of Chicago Press, 1962.

Rossman, P. *The Emerging Worldwide Electronic University: Information Age Global Higher Education.* Westport, Conn.: Greenwood Press, 1992.

Tiffin, J. W. "Telecommunications and the Trade in Teaching." *ETTI (Educational and Training Technology International)*, 1990, 27(3), 240–243.

Tiffin, J. W., and Rajasingham, L. *In Search of the Virtual Class: Education in an Information Society.* London: Routledge, 1995.

Preface

News about innovative learning partnerships in higher education and learning organizations arrives daily on our desktops. From college presidents to students, from industry leaders to government policy developers, as people learn of these partnerships they ask crucial questions:

- What do these partnerships look like?

- When and how should an institution of higher education form such a partnership?

- In the context of higher education, learning organizations, and lifelong learning, there is much talk about the "learning marketspace." What is it?

- What type of leader is needed for partnering in a learning marketspace?

- What does partnering success look like in a learning marketspace?

In the 1990s, partnerships were usually associated in most people's minds with the for-profit, corporate sector and focused primarily on complementing gaps, allying with distant partners, and outsourcing services. These strategies no longer provide a successful blueprint for partnerships in the learning marketspace. The Xerox Palo Alto Research Center (PARC) conducts Web ecology research (a new area of research examining Web development, growth, and usage patterns). PARC finds that Web markets follow what is known as the universal power law: a few large marketspaces command the majority of traffic (Adamic and Huberman, 1999). Characterized as "winner-take-all markets," these marketspaces respond to the strength, effectiveness, and attractiveness for the user that imaginative collaboration has forcefully demonstrated; these marketspaces require innovative partnerships built around and for relationships.

Partnering in the Learning Marketspace offers a blueprint to help learning institutions better understand who to partner with, why, and how. We present a conceptual framework for forming partnerships to support lifelong learners.

What Is a Learning Marketspace?

Jeffrey Rayport and John Sviokla (1994), from the Harvard Business School, coined the term *marketspace* to distinguish the new virtual world of information from the physical world of resources that we can see and touch. This shift from places to spaces is summed up in *New Rules for the New Economy* by Kevin Kelly (1998): "Place still matters, and will for a long time to come. However, the new economy operates in a 'space' rather than a place, and over time more and more economic transactions will migrate to this new space . . ." (p. 94). "People will inhabit places, but increasingly the economy inhabits a space" (p. 95).

Kelly goes on to quote Tom Peters's pronouncement, "Your worst nightmare of a competitor is now only an eighth of a second away!" through which, he says, Peters "proclaims the death of distance and the arrival of globalization" (p. 94). Rather than focusing on the nightmare of globalization, our book focuses on the potential *opportunities*, giving you a blueprint for engaging *partners*—institutions and learners—who are only an eighth of a second away.

We define the learning marketspace as an Internet gateway through which learners, employers, and learning providers are drawn together into a dynamic partnership that creates value for learners, enhances economic development, and engages institutions in meeting the needs of twenty-first century learners.[1]

From our research and involvement in developing interinstitutional virtual partnerships as well as our scholarship on demographics, construction of online learning environments, and e-mentoring, we believe the hallmark of a successful learning marketspace is the formation of partnerships between organizations in support of lifelong learning. Unfortunately, however, recent failed partnerships such as California State University's public-private California Educational Technology Initiative, and our own struggles in developing Minnesota Virtual University, illustrate lack of understanding and readiness on the part of higher education to embrace such partnerships.

Who Is This Book for?

As we suggested in the opening paragraph of this Preface, interest in partnering in a learning marketspace extends from students all the way to government policymakers. We see this book as particularly valuable for those in higher education who are concerned with developing policy and programs for a new type of lifelong learner

[1] Robert C. Heterick, Jr., and Carol Twigg are believed to have originated the term *learning marketspace* in the inaugural issue of their electronic newsletter by that name (see www.center.rpi.edu/LForum/LdfLM.html), in which they wrote: "The Learning Marketspace will focus on the 'space' of higher education, taking account of the interplay between the space and the physical world of the campus" (Heterick and Twigg, July 1, 1999).

(college presidents, deans, provosts, regents, faculty, and, of course, students in applicable departments and programs).

On the other side of the partnership, in this book we target community, government, and business leaders as well as those involved in managing and directing learning organizations, broadly defined.

What Does This Book Address?

Partnering in the Learning Marketspace addresses the gap in understanding and readiness that has characterized some recent efforts at learning partnerships by presenting a conceptual framework for developing and implementing partnerships. Organizations around the world are forming virtual partnerships as a means of projecting learning opportunities to a global audience. In the global marketspace, higher education institutions must find a way to do more than leverage their educational content by listing their courses at "education marketplace" sites. At the heart of any successful higher education institution of this new sort are a healthy set of virtual partnerships formed for promoting and sustaining lifelong learning.

We know that higher education partnerships must leverage the best content created by the partners and create a gateway to that content for learners around the world. However, to date we have missed a pressing human need: connecting e-mentors with lifelong learners. It is imperative to embrace a learning marketspace concept if we hope to engage learners with the higher education enterprise, if we hope to engage faculty with lifelong learners, and if we hope to increase the quality and quantity of e-learning and achievement.

This book focuses on the crucial questions people are asking about innovative learning partnerships: what they look like, when and how to embark on such partnerships, the type of leaders needed, and what success looks like.

What Does a Learning Marketspace Partnership Look Like?

Chapter One, "Partnerships in a Learning Marketspace," analyzes current learning marketspace partnerships in higher education. To illustrate the variety in mission and focus in partnerships serving lifelong learners, we focus on four examples:

1. Kentucky Virtual University
2. Michigan Virtual Automotive and Manufacturing College
3. UNext.com
4. Hungry Minds

Each of these partnerships has achieved considerable visibility in the higher education community and demonstrates emerging trends.

Chapter Two, "The Dynamics of Marketspace Portals," presents an in-depth analysis of portals, the "front end" of learning marketspace partnerships. We describe portal characteristics, implications for higher education partnerships, and the need to move from designing one-stop portals based on current institutional structures to creating learning marketspaces.

Chapter Three, "Priorities in a Learning Marketspace," identifies the gap between what learners need and what is currently provided by higher education. We offer priorities for partnering, and we also emphasize our institutional contract with society, note how mega-universities are working to meet the needs of lifelong learners, and describe an emerging learning marketspace partnership known as the Metro Alliance.

When and How Should an Institution Embark on a Learning Marketspace Partnership?

In Chapter Four, "Assessing Readiness for Partnerships," you will find a set of readiness criteria (compiled through our ongoing research on interinstitutional partnerships) to help your institution determine readiness for engaging in a learning marketspace partnership. Sharing results from a recent survey, we also include a concise blueprint for partnership preparation.

Chapter Five, "The Learning Marketspace Toolbox," describes three stages in developing a learning marketspace:

1. Information and access, where the partners focus on access to aggregated information about higher education and employment

2. Streamlined and shared services, where the partners define common credit transfer, registration, admissions, and other standards and procedures

3. Relationships, where the partners create knowledge through learning relationships—more specifically, through developing e-portfolios, e-mentoring, and e-learning communities

Chapter Six, "The Partnering Process: A Case Study of Minnesota Virtual University," analyzes the process of building a learning marketspace and illustrates the complexity of such an initiative. Examining a longitudinal case study of constructing the Minnesota Virtual University, we describe the practical work of building such a partnership and show how priorities, readiness criteria, and the nature of the learning marketspace as a "disruptive innovation" bear on the development process.

What Type of Leader Is Needed for Partnering in a Learning Marketspace?

Chapter Seven, "Leadership in a Global Learning Marketspace," presents a leadership model that addresses three questions:

1. What are the leadership competencies needed in a learning marketspace partnership?

2. How do you identify leaders who are authentic about partnering in a learning marketspace?

3. How do leaders manage polarity as part of partnering
   in a learning marketspace?

On this last point, it is critical for leadership to understand that to partner in a learning marketspace one must manage a variety of polarities, among them attending to emerging fringe markets as well as the mainstream needs of institutions, addressing the needs of society as a whole along with the needs of individual partners and learners, understanding how to both compete and collaborate, and balancing the need to function both globally and locally.

What Does Success Look Like in a Learning Marketspace?

We asked national and international leaders who have partnered successfully in a learning marketspace to respond to a series of questions:

- What does a successful learning marketspace partnership look like?

- How will it influence education and the educational delivery system?

- What are the most important driving forces and obstacles in building such a partnership?

- When and how should an institution embark on a partnership effort?

- What type of leader is needed?

Their insightful responses are presented as "perspectives" between chapters throughout the book.

December 2000

ANN HILL DUIN
LINDA L. BAER
DOREEN STARKE-MEYERRING

References

Adamic, L., and Huberman, B. "The Nature of Markets in the World Wide
    Web." Palo Alto, Calif.: Xerox Palo Alto Research Center, 1999.
    [ftp.parc.xerox.com/pub/dynamics/webmarkets.pdf].
Kelly, K. *New Rules for the New Economy: 10 Radical Strategies for a Connected
    World.* New York: Penguin, 1998.
Rayport, J. F., and Sviokla, J. J. "Managing in the Marketspace." *Harvard
    Business Review*, Nov.–Dec. 1994, pp. 141–150.

Acknowledgments

This book is a result of partnerships in the learning marketspace. First, we value the partnership we have developed as collaborators. Our book is a testimony to one of its core messages: that learning or making knowledge requires successful interpersonal relationships and fruitful interactions with other learners and professionals. Consequently, our endeavors to make knowledge about learning marketspaces and their implications for partnering owe much to a great variety of professional relationships.

We would like to thank Paul Wasko, Jim Bensen, and Senator Steve Kelly for their insightful comments and conversations about earlier versions of the book. We also wish to thank Mary Beth Susman and Gary Langer for helping to collect the survey data for our research on readiness criteria for partnering in the learning marketspace. We appreciate the contributions from all those who completed a survey or an interview.

Our thinking was greatly enriched by our conversations with the members of various committees and task teams with whom we have worked over the last few years to build the Minnesota Virtual University (MnVU) and the Internet System for Education and Employment Knowledge (ISEEK). Both formal meetings and informal conversations with the design team members have been invaluable to our work on this book.

We acknowledge the people who wrote perspectives and sidebars. These enriched our work with information from many experts working in the field who reflect the innovative spirit and commitment to learning that is needed in this new century.

We thank EDUCAUSE for the opportunity to write this book. We owe a great debt to the excellent work of our editors. We are particularly grateful for the professional expertise, sound advice, encouragement, and thorough work of our EDUCAUSE editor Julia Rudy.

Finally, we wish to thank our families for their tireless support and encouragement.

A.H.D.

L.L.B.

D.S.-M.

The Authors

Ann Hill Duin is associate provost and director of extended and continuing education at Iowa State University, where she leads distance education efforts and promotes and facilitates learning marketspace partnerships and integrated investment strategies. She earned her B.A. (1977) in music and English education at Luther College, Decorah, Iowa, and both her M.A. (1983) and Ph.D. (1986) at the University of Minnesota. Duin has taught at the elementary, secondary, collegiate, and corporate levels in the United States and abroad. Before joining the Iowa State University staff, she was vice provost for instructional technology and university partnerships, and professor of scientific and technical communication, at the University of Minnesota. She has published more than sixty books and journal articles and received a Distinguished Teaching Award at the University of Minnesota. She and coauthor Linda Baer regularly present at national conferences and assist education and industry in determining readiness for learning marketspace partnerships.

Linda L. Baer is senior vice chancellor for academic and student affairs at the Minnesota State Colleges and Universities System. She earned her B.A. (1970) in sociology from Washington State University, her M.A. (1975) in sociology from Colorado State University, and her Ph.D. (1983) from South Dakota State University.

Before joining the system staff, she was the senior vice president for academic and student affairs at Bemidji State University in Minnesota. Baer's publications and presentations include work in demography and rural sociology, the myths and realities of technology-enhanced education, and building virtual partnerships; she has received, among others, the Gamma Sigma Delta Outstanding Teacher Award. She serves on the Kellogg Foundation Forum for Higher Education Transformation and was on the Association of American Colleges and Universities committee that produced *Facing Change: Building the Faculty of the Future*. Duin and Baer cochaired the Minnesota Virtual University initiative.

Doreen Starke-Meyerring is a research fellow at the University of Minnesota, where she has been conducting research on the construction of the Minnesota Virtual University as a participant-observer from the beginning of its development. She has served as a member and cochair on critical task teams in the Minnesota Virtual University initiative, worked as an analyst of virtual learning environments, and published and presented on online learning. Starke-Meyerring earned her B.Ed. (1990) in Russian and English education at the University of Potsdam, Germany, and her M.A. (1993) in English at the University of North Dakota. She is currently working on her Ph.D. in rhetoric and scientific and technical communication at the University of Minnesota. Her previous experience includes teaching at the secondary and collegiate levels in Germany and in the United States, as well as developing international partnerships in higher education.

1

Partnerships in a Learning Marketspace

Call it transformation; call it a tsunami. The growth in education delivered on the Internet is occurring at digital speed, and industries are jumping in, too. According to a 1999 *New York Times* article, John T. Chambers, president and CEO of Cisco Systems, says, "The next big killer application for the Internet is going to be education. Education via the Internet is going to be so big it is going to make e-mail use look like a 'rounding error' in terms of the Internet capacity it will consume" (Friedman, 1999).

We contend that the means to riding the wave is through innovative partnerships designed to meet pressing human needs. The priorities are global and local, representing the values and cultures of organizations and individuals alike. According to Harris Bretall Sullivan and Smith LLC (2000), "With the widespread proliferation of networks and the rapid dissemination of information, the worldwide economy has been fundamentally altered. New markets are being created at a rapid pace, and old markets are being invaded by competitors that did not exist only months before. Traditional rules of competition are being altered with new models appearing and geographic and regulatory barriers disappearing" (p. 1).

For companies to succeed in the digital age, it is common for them to develop alliances with other firms within the value chain of their industry. Competitors become collaborators, and business flourishes. Innovative higher education institutions are also partnering. Through partnerships, powerful low-cost models emerge; new learning marketspaces rise from new value "webs," which replace traditional value chains (Kelly, 1998); and "the dots" (dot coms in particular) that are not weighed down by prior success (which might leave them set in their ways) enter the learning marketspace at full speed.

Here are a few examples of such partnerships:

• Hungry Minds, an Internet portal site, has partnered with the University of Maryland, UCLA Extension, Monster.com, and iVillage to offer courses and degree programs. Hungry Minds is designed to be an education site where a person can conduct research for a Ph.D. one evening and learn how to fly fish the next.

• UNext.com offers courses online with content created by the faculty of such top schools as Columbia, Stanford, Carnegie Mellon, the University of Chicago, and the London School of Economics. The partner schools control course content for the curriculum, which is marketed under the name Cardean University.

• Microsoft and MIT have formed a partnership to create educational technologies through an initiative called I-Campus, which is designing a global education system with the National University of Singapore, creating tools for large-scale collaborative engineering design projects and publishing academic works.

• The Internet education company Cenquest has partnered with the Oregon Graduate Institute, the University of Texas, Australia's University of Adelaide, and Mexico's TEC/Monterrey Tech to offer graduate business classes online to employers at more than one hundred industry sites. Students pay about $470 for each credit hour, and Cenquest shares revenues from enrollment with its partner institutions.

• Columbia University and several other highly prestigious academic centers have formed a for-profit online partnership with the

What Is a Learning Marketspace?

Learning marketspace is a carefully chosen term designed to convey a new interface between learning providers, learners, and the organizations with whom they affiliate. To get a sense of the physical manifestation, begin with a comprehensive Web presence open to the world, serving as a vast repository for educational material.

One feature of this marketspace is its summary of the material and index of content, which helps the learner who is conducting a search determine the site's relevance so he or she can, with a high degree of confidence, find the learning opportunities that match his or her need. Another feature is provision of an entire map of the subject area that learners are interested in, for use once they find their target.

Now add to the marketspace the institutional faculty and research facilities as well as professional and membership associations in each specific discipline embraced by the marketspace. Each entity makes a contribution to the repository to synthesize a knowledge domain made up of a database and tools. Each participates in designing and operating the knowledge domain, contributing to it and deriving benefit from it. Because the learning marketspace brings together an entire knowledge domain in a scholarly community, it provides the nexus for scholarly dialogue, vetting of research, standards of performance, certificates of completion, and so forth.

Finally, enter the *learners.* They can search the many domains for the knowledge they seek. Once they identify a domain, they can fully explore the information, data, tools, techniques, curriculum, research, and processes that are available from all the participants. The learning marketspace provides a consistent interface, as well as services common to all participating entities.

MICHAEL G. DOLENCE
Michael G. Dolence and Associates

New York Public Library, the British Library, the Smithsonian Institution's National Museum of Natural History, the London School of Economics and Political Science, and Cambridge University Press. The goal of the company, which is called Fathom.com, is to provide knowledge in its broadest form: "Classes taught by prominent academics like the historian Simon Schama, reference books like the Cambridge Dictionary of Philosophy, interviews with people like Dorothy Parker and Frank Lloyd Wright from Columbia's oral history archive, and documents like [the] Magna Carta" (Arenson, 2000).

When established institutions embark on such a learning marketspace partnership, stakeholders' emotional reactions vary. Some are tremendously excited because they recognize the institution's need to partner in order to develop online programs and resources for learners. These people are for the most part genuinely ready to collaborate with colleagues at other institutions to meet the needs of learners. Other stakeholders genuinely fear that online resources resulting from partnerships represent a second-class form of learning. A third group of stakeholders are suspicious, believing such partnerships are just the next ineffective educational scheme, competition for scarce resources, additional burden without reward, a top-down decision forced upon them, or simply another nuisance keeping them from conducting research or other activities.

This variety of concerns became evident in interviews we held with stakeholders involved in developing Minnesota Virtual University. Reactions included the desire to control both the partnership and the content developed. This fear of loss of control stems in part from a focus on the conventional, physical notion of markets, as opposed to the new marketspace thinking. As we mentioned in the Preface, Rayport and Sviokla (1994) from the Harvard Business School coined the term *marketspace* to distinguish the new virtual world of information from the physical world of resources. "A space, unlike a place, is an electronically created environment," says

Kevin Kelly in *New Rules for the New Economy*. "It is where more and more of the economy happens. Unlike place, space has unlimited dimensions. Entities (people, objects, agents, bits, nodes, etc.) can be adjacent in a thousand different ways and a thousand different directions" (1998, p. 95). Because of the multiple connections, the hallmark of an electronic space is its relationships: "The advantage of spaces is rooted less in their nongeographical virtuality and more in their unlimited ability to absorb connections and relationships. By means of communications, network spaces can connect all kinds of nodes, dimensions, relationships, and interactions—not just those physically close to one another" (p. 96).

Notable among the relationships being redefined as the network economy moves from places to spaces are those defined as being with competitors.

Instead of focusing on fear of competition, we prefer to emphasize opportunities in partnerships. We define the learning marketspace as an Internet gateway through which learners, employers, and education providers are drawn together into a dynamic partnership that creates value for learners, enhances economic development, and engages institutions in meeting the needs of twenty-first-century learners.

Learning Marketspace Partnerships: The Landscape

We begin our exploration of this new landscape of educational partnering by highlighting four marketspace partnerships—Kentucky Virtual University, Michigan Virtual Automotive and Manufacturing College, UNext.com, and Hungry Minds—to illustrate how each represents a distinct mission and focus in terms of partnering to serve learners. Each example has achieved considerable visibility in the higher education community and demonstrates trends that have begun to take shape in the development of learning marketspace partnerships.

A Partnership Grid

In the scholarship on academic administration and leadership, partnerships designed to offer learning over the Internet have been classified in a number of ways: the degree of institutional integration (Smith, 1998), organizational structure (Hanna, 1998), governance structure (Hurst, 1998), economic basis and scope (Athey, 1998), and the extent to which innovative technology is used (Michel, 1998).

Among these systems of classification, Smith's system focuses on higher education consortia formed to exploit the potential of communications technologies in permitting scheduling flexibility, variety of courses and degrees, and educational value. Smith believes such consortia are an effective basis for mega-universities and categorizes them according to three images suggesting the level of institutional integration: the course broker, the collaborator, and the wholesale purchaser.

Hurst's six virtual university scenarios—open university, governor's university, virtual community college and university, institutional competition and consumer advocacy, coordinated collaboration, and current structure—help colleges and universities evaluate particular structures and governance models for distance learning.

Given the hundreds of such partnerships being created today, here we present a simple grid that is useful in understanding and "positioning" them according to their fundamental or distinctive attributes. To illustrate, four current partnerships are placed on a grid (Figure 1.1) according to whether each is primarily a corporate or a public entity and whether it serves principally a specific or a general audience.

Corporate-Targeted

The controlling interest in a corporate-targeted partnership is commercial; that is, the partnership entity is a dot com. As a targeted

Figure 1.1. A Learning Marketspace Partnership Grid

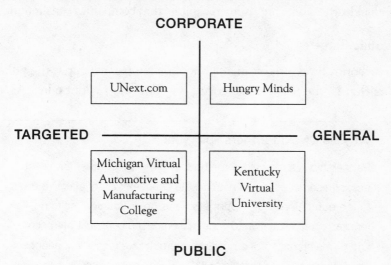

entity, it focuses on specific groups of corporate learners and issues invitations to institutions with the cultural capital to match these expectations. This type of partnership is particularly new for higher education in that the corporation holds controlling interest in the outcomes.

Beginning with the upper-left quadrant of Figure 1.1, we have as an example UNext.com (www.unext.com). It represents a corporate entity targeted to private companies, and business education broadly. Partners include faculty from schools such as Columbia, Stanford, Carnegie Mellon, the University of Chicago, and the London School of Economics. According to the company's Web site in May 2000, their mission was to "serve those who understand that thriving in today's competitive knowledge-based economy demands a continual advancement in their knowledge and skills" and "to provide companies, and the individuals who work for them, the most effective means possible to increase their human capital." Their goal was "to create powerful learning communities that marry the world's most respected academic scholars and institutions with the global reach and interactive capabilities of the Internet." The

UNext.com focus is on scholars, institutions, and technology; individual learners here are "human capital" that companies can "retain."

Public-Targeted

The controlling interest in a public-targeted partnership is the public; that is, the partnership entity is a "dot org" or "dot edu." As a

---

Why Do UNext Partnerships Work?

Partnership is a marvelous method for bringing together the variety of expertise necessary to perform the complex task of effective distance education. But a partnership is not a magical solution. It requires careful attention to construction, to the continual interaction, and to maintenance of a positive, interactive, effective experience. The UNext.com partnership, with its consortium of leading educational institutions, works for several reasons:

- We have tailored the relationship to ensure the highest-quality interaction among ourselves, assigning final approval of the quality of all our courses, from inception through delivery, to the universities in the consortium.

- We target students who would otherwise not attend a university; that is, we complement the activities of our consortium partners.

- We couple our pedagogical expertise with the academic-content expertise of our partners, each party offering essential components that the other lacks to produce effective courses. UNext has disaggregated the traditional academic model. One group of people determines content, another constructs a course, and yet another delivers the material, coaches, and interacts with the students.

- We follow a constructivist learning approach of inquiry whereby each course topic is structured around a realistic problem that students must address. Such problem-based, interactive learning has targeted entity, it focuses on a relatively specific set of lifelong learn-ers and key industries in a region. The rationale is not directly com-mercial; rather, it is intended to help the public or the state as a whole. It is based on a state or region's economic development plan. This type of partnership is closely aligned to the many efforts of conventional providers of vocational education. If an institution is

---

the power to motivate, direct the learning, and produce far more effective mastery of the material than the more traditional class-room does.

- UNext provides the financial and personnel resources that a uni-versity cannot afford; expertise in the underlying delivery tech-nologies and pedagogies; and the dedicated concentration of people who develop, test, deliver, and monitor the quality of the educational experience with twenty-four/seven reliability and ser-vice. A traditional university is simply not configured to carry out all these ancillary activities; nor should it be.

- Finally, the partnership includes the companies and students who use our courses: for these people, we promise useful rewards in return for their time and effort. We create a social community that covers a wide range of topics, from debates on course material to discussions of timely world events related to the class topics, and discussions of everyday life.

Our experience has worked quite well, but only because UNext is dedicated to pedagogical excellence, because we work closely with our academic partners, and because we respect one another's contri-butions and abilities. Without such respect, the partnership would fail.

DON NORMAN
President, Learning Systems
(a Division of UNext.com)

in a state that has an economic development plan, such a partnership has a greater chance to succeed.

We place the example of what was originally, in 1996, called Michigan Virtual Automotive College (MVAC) in the lower-left quadrant. This nonprofit entity presents as its targeted mission statement: "The Michigan Virtual Automotive College will capitalize on emerging distance learning technology to provide high-quality, convenient, and cost-effective automotive training and education throughout the state. By creating a strategic link between education and industry, MVAC will ensure an efficient and effective educational response to the rapidly changing needs of Michigan's leading industry" (www.mvac.org/mission.html, Dec. 2000).

This partnership between Michigan's public colleges and universities and the auto industry was changed in 1999 to include manufacturing and renamed Michigan Virtual Automotive and Manufacturing College (MVAMC). Most recently, MVAMC has become a division of Michigan Virtual University (MVU), yet it still exists as a separate entity with its own Internet domain name.

Partners in MVU include the Michigan Community College Virtual Learning Collaborative (twenty-eight institutions), the Michigan Economic Development Corporation, Michigan Association for Computer-Related Technology Users in Learning, the Society of Manufacturing Engineers (SME), the Michigan Education Policy Fellowship Program, Eastern Michigan University, and Ford Motor Company.

According to this group, the partnership enjoys the advantage of having resources to support preparing students for employment; resources and teacher training for anytime, anywhere learning; continuing research on industry employee training needs and best practices in distance learning; and statewide, national, and international markets.

In contrast to many state virtual university efforts, Michigan Virtual University is funded as an entity that is separate from the Michigan higher education system. This was a strategic move on the part of the state to enable a virtual entity to serve the entire state at its maximum capacity, to be able to move quickly and be responsive to critical state needs, and to remain separate from direct control of the resources on the part of existing institutions.

Public-General

In a public-general partnership, once again the controlling interest is the public, resulting in a dot org or dot edu entity. The focus is on increasing access to citizens, with attention to maximizing all citizens' skills and educational level and addressing emerging skill needs. This type of partnership is most closely aligned with traditional institutions. Those involved need a clear commitment to revising policies and removing barriers to citizen access to education.

We place our example, Kentucky Virtual University (KYVU), in the lower-right quadrant because this entity's mission is to be "a student-centered, technology-based system for coordinating the delivery of postsecondary education that meets the needs of citizens and employers across the Commonwealth." The Kentucky Virtual University's goal is to function as a clearinghouse for distance learning opportunities provided by both in-state and out-of-state institutions, to offer competency-based credentialing, and to afford a single point of access to student, library, and academic support services statewide (www.kyvu.org, Dec. 2000).

The nonprofit KYVU is a cooperative among Kentucky's existing postsecondary institutions, an agreement based on the Kentucky Postsecondary Education Improvement Act. The partnering institutions have these responsibilities:

- Participating with KYVU in identifying the post-secondary education needs of the citizens and employers in the Commonwealth
- Identifying and developing distance learning courses, programs, and other credentialing mechanisms that are responsive to the identified needs and that are

consistent with institutional missions and the statewide
Strategic Agenda

- Reducing inefficiencies and improving quality in
  course and program offerings through interinstitutional
  cooperation, the use of distance learning technologies,
  and the application of contemporary instructional
  technologies

- Identifying or developing high-quality distance learning courses and programs that are competitive in the
  national and international market

- Providing coordinated student, library, and academic
  support services for KYVU that meet the unique needs
  of KYVU students

- Participating in the KYVU consistent with adopted
  policies and the statutory responsibilities of each
  institution [www.kyvu.org, Dec. 2000]

The goals and responsibilities are similar to those of partners
involved in other state or public-initiated virtual universities,
notably California Virtual Campus, Minnesota Virtual University,
Southern Regional Electronic Campus, Globewide Network Academy, and Western Governors University. Although Western Governors University states that it does not wish to be "just another
distance learning content broker," according to the criteria of our
grid it falls squarely within the lower-right quadrant since its mission is largely public and for a general audience. WGU's distin-
guishing feature continues to be its focus on competencies as
opposed to credits, along with a massive number of national and
international partners.

Some individual institutions of the sort in this category of
public-general have also worked to extend access to their offerings.

The University of Maryland's University College (UMUC) and UCLA Extension are two examples.

UMUC has both a statewide mission—"to extend access to post-secondary educational opportunities for individuals who combine work with study, with a special emphasis on Maryland's professional workforce education needs"—and a global mission—"to sustain international eminence by extending access to American post-secondary degrees and non-credit programs worldwide" (www.umuc.edu/gen/vision.html, Dec. 2000).

Both UCLA Extension and UMUC have partnered or developed corporate spin-offs. OnlineLearning.net, for instance, has rights to put forty-nine hundred UCLA Extension courses online and has published nearly nine hundred in the past four years. Corporate spin-offs and partnerships of this kind move their Internet learning efforts far closer to those of the final quadrant of our partnership grid, as seen in the example of the corporate-but-general orientation of Hungry Minds.

Corporate-General

The controlling interest in the corporate-general type of partnership is commercial. Instead of focusing on a specific group of corporate learners, the audience is all online learners. Although the interest of this dot com is certainly commercial, the focus is more on personal enrichment and education from a continuum of online learning providers as opposed to a select few. Of the four quadrants, this one is the most open in that it is not limited to a particular state, industry, or set of corporate learners. This type of dot com–dot edu partnership is the most flexible for both learner and provider. We place our example of Hungry Minds in this quadrant.

The focus on a general audience is expressed in the banner description on the company's Web site (www.hungryminds.com): "Welcome to Hungry Minds. . . . Where complicated subjects become simple. Where the book meets the Web. Where your computer is your classroom. Where learning is easier than ever. Dig in."

The goal is to help learners learn "anything anytime." This can take the form of demand for a quick class on managing, a chat room, or an academic course from a highly regarded public or private organization. Given its broader audience—distance learners in general—the Hungry Minds site is presented in the spirit of fun, enjoyment, social interaction, and quality in learning. This approach distinguishes Hungry Minds from the other three groups of partnership entities, which focus mostly on the information and skills aspect of knowledge and learning rather than on the integration with the social and emotional aspects of learning. As such, Hungry Minds represents a brave step in the learning marketspace. Consequently, its Web site (www.hungryminds.com) abounds with opportunities for learners to connect with each other as well as with guides and experts.

Hungry Minds also shares its strategies for partnering with institutions, bridging the cultural gap between scholars and the Internet: (1) contracts stay simple; (2) they are nonexclusive, meaning schools may exit easily if they get cold feet; and (3) contracts are flexible. Institutions that want to create more complex partnerships or deepen their relationships with Hungry Minds are encouraged to do so (Berinato, 2000).

Learning Marketspaces: Transition to Portals

Although the mission and focus of a partnership represent the heart and soul of the endeavor, a partnership's front end most often takes the form of a portal (the "entry point" from which the user goes on to any number of Web pages). Reflecting general developments of Internet structuring processes, learning marketspaces also commonly present themselves as a portal featuring links to the partners' sites and other resources. In Chapter Two we present an analysis of portals, noting the important development that occurs as they move from a function of sustaining existing institutional processes to one of engaging learners in new ways.

References

Arenson, K. W. "Columbia in Web Venture to Share Learning for Profit." *New York Times*, Mar. 3, 2000.

Athey, T. "Non-Traditional Universities Challenge 21st Century Higher Education." *On the Horizon*, 1998, 6(5), 5–7. [www.camfordpublishing.com/oth/archive/98/vol6_no5a.htm].

Berinato, S. "Coming After You: HungryMinds.com—It's Not Just an Internet Portal, It's a New Way to Think." *University Business*, March 2000. [www.universitybusiness.com/0003/hungry.html].

Friedman, T. L. "Foreign Affairs: Next, It's E-ducation." *New York Times*, Nov. 17, 1999.

Hanna, D. "Higher Education in an Era of Digital Competition: Emerging Organizational Models." *Journal of Asynchronous Learning Networks*, 1998, 2(1). [www.aln.org/alnweb/journal/vol2_issue1/hanna.htm].

Harris Bretall Sullivan and Smith, LLC. *The Network Economy*. San Francisco: Harris Bretall Sullivan and Smith, 2000. [www.hbss.com/netecon.pdf].

Hurst, F. "So You Want to Start a Virtual University?" *On the Horizon*, 1998, 6(4), 4–8. [www.camfordpublishing.com/oth/archive/98/vol6_no4a.htm].

Kelly, K. *New Rules for the New Economy: 10 Radical Strategies for a Connected World*. New York: Penguin, 1998.

Michel, J. "Engineering Education Towards Virtual Universities." Text for the Conferences on Virtual Universities in Budapest and in Prague, written in Aug. 1998. [www.paris.enpc.fr/~michel-j/publi/JM310.html].

Rayport, J. F., and Sviokla, J. J. "Managing in the Marketspace." *Harvard Business Review*, Nov.–Dec. 1994, pp. 141–150.

Smith, B. "Creating Consortia: Export the Best, Import the Rest." *Converge Magazine*, Dec. 1998. [www.convergemag.com/Publications/CNVGDec98/highered/highered.shtml].

2

The Dynamics of
Marketspace Portals

When talk turns to portals, even among those who are familiar with the Internet, people often appear confused, and rightly so. We have found no analysis of portals as they are currently understood that we consider clear enough for reproduction here. But because efforts to serve today's learners often assume the form of a portal, an analysis of this "front end" to the partnership entities described in Chapter One and its implications for partnership clearly is needed to better understand a learning marketspace, or LMS.

Michael B. Quinion, author of the site "World Wide Words," attributes first use of the word *portal* to Netscape, applied to "a Web site that is the first point of access on the World Wide Web, usually the site associated with the *Home* button on the user's browser" (www.quinion.com/words/turnsofphrase). Quinion calls attention to two aspects of the move to portal sites. First, owning and controlling a widely used entry point entails considerable financial advantage in selling advertising space and dealing in other services that the user sees upon entry. Second, the portal site becomes a "honeypot," that is, it attracts "all sorts of other facilities and [becomes] a focus around which online communities can form." The example of Yahoo! comes to mind, functioning as a gateway to other sites, the venue for the popular search engine of the same name, a free e-mail system, and an entire community of Yahoo! services and consumers of those services.

The higher education version of a portal conventionally takes the form of the ubiquitous "one-stop," merging student services, personal organizers, courses, schedules, and the like. Although these one-stops are logical and easy to navigate, they are created expressly to streamline business processes. Therefore they remain institution-centered, mainly reproducing on the Web current institutional structures and processes. Links to offices and services rarely entice the learner to stay at a one-stop longer than is absolutely necessary.

In contrast, a learning marketspace portal serves to engage learners through attention to relationships. In this chapter, we define and classify portals, noting in particular the educational implications in aggregating learners to fewer and fewer portal sites.

Defining a Portal

Portals are relatively new Internet technologies that are increasingly replacing the home page as a gateway to the Internet. There is little consensus on how to define *portal*, what purpose a portal serves, how it is structured, and how it in turn structures education on the Internet.

The concept of the portal depends to some extent on the community that is using it. Business communities tend to have a different view of portals than do educational institutions. In short, the "portal landscape" varies widely and, beyond what Quinion's rather brief explanation proposes, is vaguely defined. It represents only the beginning of what may be called the structuring and organizing phase of cyberspace frontier settlements.

Since the portal is a relatively recent development, analysis or research on the subject is scarce. In technology magazines, a portal is variously described as the next generation of online services; or the old formula of content, community, and core services (such as e-mail) but in a new package, hence a trim Web interface; or a gateway to Internet access; or a hub to locate Web content that people commonly need.

The technical difference between a home page and a portal, then, is mostly in the quality of the integration of content, community, and communication services and the extent to which these services and resources are adjusted to users. Although the home page essentially offers the same content and services for all users—following the maxim that one size fits all—a portal presents the opportunity to customize or personalize these services to users' needs. The portal takes into account the different ways in which people work, look for information, and use services. As Howard Strauss (2000), manager of academic applications at Princeton University, explains, home pages are owner-centered, but portals tend to be user-centered.

The Current Portal Landscape

The varied purposes for the portal center on three themes: convenience, revenue creation, and efficiency. These are interrelated and in many cases difficult to separate from one another. To better understand them, we offer three taxonomies.

Convenience and Revenue: The Horizontal Portal

The original portal sites—ISPs (Internet service providers) and search engines—are often referred to as *horizontal portals*. They tend to serve an array of audiences; consequently, they offer a great variety of information along with some opportunity for personalization (for example, allowing the user to adjust the appearance, layout, or content of the site to personal preferences), but less customization (say, providing or selecting specific content on the basis of user preference). For the most part, these portals still consist of search engines as well as categories of links to various information and service resources on the Web. Directed at audiences outside of the organization, these portals offer little in-depth customization. Partnerships in this case are largely driven by the desire to offer more "features" to attract more visitors.

Efficiency: The Vertical Portal

In contrast to a horizontal portal, a *vertical portal* tends to serve a known audience, such as a single organization, to improve efficiency and productivity. This is the one-stop we have already mentioned. It helps the organization function more efficiently by allowing students or employees to take care of much of their business from just one access point. Consequently, a vertical portal provides specialized—and usually customized—content and services, often pursuing depth rather than breadth. Given the focus on a specific audience, a vertical portal is often linked to a database with information known to be relevant to the well-defined user.

According to Strauss, access to different databases makes a vertical portal expensive and complex because it requires extensive collaboration and often standardization of highly sensitive data. Additional costs include maintaining the portal and training personnel in using it. Especially with regard to college and university portals, Strauss argues that large amounts of money can be saved if institutions could be persuaded to collaborate in these efforts.

Despite the complexity, expense, and potential difficulties in building portals, they tend not to disrupt the organization in any fundamental way if they are built in isolation by one institution in order to streamline its existing processes. This is not to say that these portals do not entail discontinuity or radical change within an organization; in fact, they often do because they require numerous departments to communicate with each other. Nevertheless, these portals typically exhibit the tendency of what Harvard Business School professor Clayton Christensen (1997) calls "sustaining technologies" to "improve the performance of established products, along the dimensions of performance that mainstream customers in major markets have historically valued" (p. xv). A one-stop portal, for instance, clearly improves the performance of the college or university in a way that traditional students value; with it, they can register for courses, find financial aid, and access their grades efficiently.

Partnership and Relationship: The Marketspace Portal

Partnering organizations have recently begun to build *marketspace portals*, which are designed to develop and maintain relationships. These relationship-oriented efforts do not merely improve the efficiency of existing ways of learning; they represent an entirely new structure—a new marketspace in which learning occurs. Visible examples of such marketspaces in U.S. higher education are America's Learning Exchange, Western Governors University, Kentucky Virtual University, Michigan Virtual University, and the Southern Regional Electronic Campus.

These learning marketspaces are intended to open large markets of online learners rather than to streamline the processes of an individual institution. Thus they are likely to exhibit the tendency associated with what Christensen (p. xv) calls "disruptive technologies" to "result in worse product performance, at least in the near-term," as distinguished from sustaining technologies, which immediately improve performance for the mainstream market. In his study of the impact of technological innovation on certain industries, he found that this second type of technological change actually "disrupted or redefined performance trajectories—and consistently resulted in the failure of the industry's leading firms" (p. 9). He provides examples, such as the 5.25-inch drive in the disk-drive industry, hydraulic excavators in the mechanical excavator industry, and discount retailers in the traditional chain and department store businesses. Another, perhaps better-known, example is that of the personal computer setting new performance expectations in the mainframe industry.

Such is the disruptive potential of the innovation that is just beginning to take shape in the online education marketspace.

Despite attempts to design features in response to the needs of the lifelong learner (as opposed to, say, the late-teens, on-campus learner), most emerging marketspace portals still exhibit institutional structures that have persisted in failing to genuinely meet these needs (see Chapter Three). In short, learners who are now coming online in accelerating numbers represent part of an "e-cology" that is—in the classic pattern of disruptive versus sustaining technologies—still little understood by mainstream institutions in U.S. higher education. The key to understanding the dynamics of a marketspace portal is the environment, or e-cology, in which this portal exists.

The E-cology of Marketspace Portals

By the end of 1999, roughly 120 million users had connected to the Internet in the United States alone ("Nielsen//Netratings Report . . . ," 2000), with the number expected to reach 177 million by 2003 ("Internet Users . . . ," 1999). The number of worldwide Internet users in 1999 is expected to double by 2002 ("The World's Online Populations," 2000).

A growing number of businesses follow this surging number of Internet users, with e-commerce generating more than $500 billion in revenue in 1999 (Dembeck, 1999). By 2003, e-commerce revenue is expected to grow to $1.3 trillion ("Internet Commerce . . . ," 1999).

Similar trends are predicted for the education sector. With the growing demand for lifelong learning in the digital age, Internet users will request much of that learning online and expect it to be delivered in flexible ways. Current estimates point to more than 100 million learners enrolling in online courses by 2004. These numbers will only rise further when the Internet is wireless and all the more mobile.

These trends are accompanied by restructuring processes that shape the characteristics and dynamics of the learning marketspace. First, with more than six trillion bytes of text, the Web rivals the Library of Congress in size—yet it does not have a decent card catalogue. As a consequence, searching has become increasingly frustrating. This fosters high demand for shaped, structured, customized, and personalized Web experiences, a demand that portals of various kinds have been attempting to address. Portals have grown in popularity, with sites such as Yahoo! commanding almost half of all Web traffic at the end of 1999 ("Nielsen//Netratings Reports . . . ," 2000).

Second, as the Internet enters the next phase of its development, user behavior continues to mature. Rather than merely a fun and interesting novelty, the Web is viewed as a tool to be used repeatedly to meet daily needs. Users develop search paths and return to those sites that have been most helpful in meeting their needs. The result is that the Web is taking on a distinct shape—at least in the eyes of users. The "Nielsen//Netratings Report on Internet Year 1999," for example, showed that although the number of users increased 27 percent over the course of that year, and the time spent online per month per person increased more than 10 percent, users visited fewer unique sites though they viewed more pages: "The number of unique sites visited per month in the beginning of the year decreased 40 percent from fifteen to nine sites in December, while the number of page views seen per surfing session increased 68 percent from nineteen to thirty-two during the same period." The study attributes these trends to the increasing maturity of both the medium and the users. In short, ever-fewer megasites attract an ever-larger portion of Web traffic.

Recent Xerox PARC research on Web e-cology shows that these trends are not accidental. Quite the opposite: they reflect the laws that now govern the Internet. Adamic and Huberman (1999) studied distributions and surfing patterns of sixty thousand users at 120,000 Web sites and found that "a large number of sites command the traffic of a large segment of the Web population" (p. 3). Such a disproportionate channeling of user volume among sites is characteristic of "winner-take-all markets, wherein the top few contenders capture a significant part of the market share" (p. 3). The startling trend is toward aggregation: 1 percent of all the sites examined attracted more than half of all user volume; and 5 percent of sites accounted for 75 percent of user volume. Educational (dot edu) sites reflect the same pattern. Here, the researchers found that the top 5 percent of the educational sites attracted roughly 60 percent of visitor traffic (Adamic and Huberman, 1999).

One might say that individual mom-and-pop portals are attracting fewer and fewer visitors, while successful mega marketspace portals attract the majority of the entire population on the Web. Or, using the popular analogy of the Internet as a frontier, we might summarize this trend by saying that the "homesteading phase" of the Internet—in which every person or organization has its own home page or even its own one-stop portal, and perhaps a relatively equal chance of attracting visitors—is coming to a close. Internet development now is less about homesteading than about building towns and marketspaces, including general as well as targeted ones.

Any partnership, then, attempting to build an LMS must be aware that it is dealing with a winner-take-all e-cology, which raises the stakes for establishing a successful partnership. Such an alliance is not simply about working together from existing structures but instead building an entirely new, and surely disruptive, structure. A college or university has three choices: (1) stay at its homestead; (2) disperse, and pay rent for space in someone else's marketspace; or (3) partner to build an LMS. Whatever the choice, the implications are great.

Implications for Partnerships in Higher Education

The implications stemming from the current Internet e-cology are profound. If a state or region intends to retain and attract prosperous information and high-technology industries, it needs to offer an appropriate learning infrastructure—in other words, a learning marketspace with a dominant brand name for digital-age learning. Individual higher education portals, with all their idiosyncrasies, no longer constitute an efficient infrastructure for a digital-age learning organization or for citizens in general.

Furthermore, if the needs of diverse learners are to be addressed, including those learners previously excluded from educational communities, then higher education partnerships and their accompanying portals must become portals in a double sense. First, they must be developed and sustained through partnership to offer the greatest variety of courses, resources, and services to their learners. Second, this spirit of partnership for learning must extend to the learners themselves. The foremost goal of a partnership and a portal of this kind should be to build a relationship—a learning partnership between learners and learners and between learners and "e-mentors." (An *e-mentor* is an individual or a group of individuals at an institution whose task is to guide a learner in achieving his or her goals. The word *learner* refers, for our purposes, to an individual or to a business, industry, or citizen group.)

None of the education partnerships and accompanying portals that we have examined to date has reached this level of engagement. Recent additions to the dot com world have begun to address the need for some kind of e-mentor. For example, icontact.com, recently merged with !hey software, offers several solutions for engaging customers, such as interactive voice responses and on-request chat. Similar communication technologies can be used to engage learners in a learning marketspace.

From Mainstream to Marketspace

Though the current level of engagement is limited, we believe that institutions can partner wisely for the purposes of engaging learners and attending to their contract with society and individual learners. To describe this concept further, we present in Table 2.1 a comparison of means by which an institution can move toward engaging in an LMS partnership and envisioning a portal that works to change how the world learns. A mainstream portal improves existing performance, whereas an LMS portal sets new performance trajectories.

As is true of the entire World Wide Web, higher education partnerships and their accompanying portals are in a continuous state of rapid prototyping (see Schrage, 2000). The left column in Table 2.1 presents portals largely as we currently envision them in higher education; that is, they help learners work within the structural and social constraints of the institution. Despite bringing together a wealth of student services into a one-stop environment, these portals maintain a decidedly institutional focus.

In contrast, the right column in the table shows that the marketspace portal promotes interpersonal learning experiences by con-

Table 2.1. Moving from Mainstream to Learning Marketspace Portals

Mainstream Portal	Marketspace Portal
Institutional focus (the institution focuses on making navigation of its site easier)	Learner focus (the learner and mentor focus on making their needs clearer)
Convenience-based	Relationship-based
Increase in information	Increase in e-literacy
Authority	Adaptation
Resources	Risk
Reactive	Proactive
Access	Engagement
Cooperation	Collaboration, commitment, covenant
Public (one to many)	Private (one to one)
Advice and advising	Connections and long-term mentoring
Example plans	Evolving portfolios

necting learners to each other and to e-mentors, and by helping learners build strategic learning portfolios best suited to their needs. Often taking the form of a disruptive technology and thus requiring organizational learning and change, a learning marketspace portal may initially result in poorer performance in mainstream markets. But the features of the disruptive technology that the fringe customers value, in the case of lifelong learning, are engagement, collaboration, commitment, and mentoring.

An institution's traditional customers—resident learners—initially may not prefer an LMS portal; in fact, the concept may well be embraced only by the least-profitable customers—in higher education, the distance learners (Archer, Garrison, and Anderson, 1999). According to Christensen (1997), most companies with a practiced discipline of listening to their best customers and identifying new products that promise greater profitability and growth are rarely able to build a case for investing in disruptive technologies until it is too late or they have lost significant market share. What is perhaps most difficult, then, about building an LMS portal is that it cannot be limited to reproducing current institutional structures and processes; rather, it requires organizational learning and change.

Furthermore, the portal of a learning marketspace works to integrate educational offerings from different types of organizations. As such, the portal usually appears inferior to that of a traditional university because it does not (yet) deliver a full range of services, such as registration, admissions, community events, learning support services, and so forth. Developing the full potential of an LMS portal takes time because the portal shows its full potential only through relationship building and standardizing processes among the partnering organizations. Since each organization has its unique structure, culture, and traditions, such standardization processes are complex and challenging.

The LMS partnerships highlighted in Chapter One indicate movement toward greater engagement with learners. Hungry Minds offers multiple ways for learners to connect to each other, learn about various topics, take a course, or contact subject experts to discuss specific subject matter. The focus here is on multiple forms of interaction between learners' "hungry minds." Beyond simply allowing access to existing opportunities, the site provides additional ways for learners to connect in the spirit of fun, enjoyment, social interaction, and quality in learning.

Nevertheless, the LMS portal at this point has not been fully applied by any one partnership entity. Although each of the partnerships we highlight in this book has a standardized format for listing courses, the learner is then sent off to individual institutions, where he or she must deal with their standards, norms, and service conditions. No standardized format makes it easier for the learner to compare courses; no organizational database is tapped; no organizational structure is challenged. Although collaboration between learners and between experts and learners is encouraged, no similar collaboration among the institutional partners enjoys comparable inducement yet. This critical missing piece of interorganizational collaboration makes it difficult to help the learner build a strategic learning portfolio. Thus, today the partnering site must still focus on one-time opportunity, which—although engaging—does not yet deliver a strategic learning experience.

The Leap

Moving from current one-stop to LMS portals demands nothing short of a leap. Established giants in the higher education enterprise may have the greatest difficulty in moving beyond the one-stop, "sustaining" portal to embrace a "disruptive" portal that at first hardly promises to be successful. But nothing less than establishing human-to-human connections—at the interinstitutional and individual levels—is needed if we intend to address critical gaps between a traditional focus on institutional structures and learner needs as those needs emerge in the digital age.

References

Adamic, L., and Huberman, B. "The Nature of Markets in the World Wide Web." Palo Alto, Calif.: Xerox Palo Alto Research Center, 1999. [ftp://ftp.parc.xerox.com/pub/dynamics/webmarkets.pdf].

Archer, W. D., Garrison, R., and Anderson, T. "Adopting Disruptive Technologies in Traditional Universities: Continuing Education as an Incubator for Innovation." *DEOSNEWS,* 1999, 9(11). [www.ed.psu.edu/acsde/deos/deosnews/deosnews9_11.asp].

Christensen, C. M. *The Innovator's Dilemma: When New Technologies Cause Great Firms to Fail.* Boston: Harvard Business School Press, 1997.

Dembeck, C. "U.S. E-Commerce Soars by 127 Percent." *E-Commerce Times,* Oct. 27, 1999. [www.ecommercetimes.com/news/articles/991027–5.shtml].

"Internet Commerce Climbs to $1.3 Trillion by 2003, Users to Total 500 Million." *Edupage,* Sept. 29, 1999.

"Internet Users Now Exceed 100 Million." *Edupage,* Nov. 12, 1999.

"Nielsen//Netratings Reports on Internet Year 1999 in Review." Jan. 20, 2000. [www.nielsen-netratings.com/press_releases/pr_000120_review.htm].

Schrage, M. *Serious Play: How the World's Best Companies Stimulate to Innovate.* Boston: Harvard Business School Press, 2000.

Strauss, H. "What Is a Web Portal?" Corporation for Research and Educational Networking (CREN), *Tech Talk with the Experts.* Audiocast, Jan. 20, 2000. [www.cren.net/know/techtalk/events/portals.html].

"The World's Online Populations." Cyberatlas. July 28, 2000. [cyberatlas.internet.com/big_picture/geographics/article/0,1323,5911_151151,00.html].

Perspective: Jaap Tuinman

A successful learning marketspace partnership looks like any other successful partnership: each partner must benefit sufficiently so that it is a winner or can think of itself that way. No other kind of partnership endures. So the key is to ensure that the various interests of learners, employers, and providers mesh. In practice, the local context may vary, but in general one can make certain observations.

First, learners want from a partnership credibility, choice, service, and price; that is to say, learners need to know that the credential they earn has value—in the workplace and in terms of future advancement (academic or otherwise). Second, the learner of the future will not eat at the prototypical one-hamburger McDonald's. Of course, the good people who make the Big Mac figured this out quite some time ago. Open texture (multiple pathways, multiple options) is the watchword. Third, learners want service; they have suffered too much from inattention to their needs in traditional learning institutions. These learners want service now—to the point, courteous, with a minimum of fuss. Price is an issue, but it is not the dominant one. With awareness of choice comes awareness of difference in quality—and willingness to pay more, if the value is there.

Influence on Education

An LMS partnership will influence the educational delivery system only indirectly. The emergence of such partnerships is a result of a number of fundamental developments: shifting to a knowledge economy, erupting digital power, all-encompassing opportunities in communications, and so forth. It is these developments that confront traditional notions of education and traditional educational delivery systems. At base, *every* known educational concept is open to reanalysis; this includes the very notion of education, as well as the more trivial need to tear apart and redefine such matters as courses, credits, skills, classes, degrees, and so forth.

Driving Forces and Obstacles

Considering the driving forces and obstacles in building a partnership returns us to the basic motivation of the partners involved. The customer, the consumer—or her legal guardian—constitutes one of the key drivers. Henry Ford wanted all of us to drive black cars, but Ms. Sally didn't, so it wasn't long before colorful cars hit the road. Once parents and students begin to fully understand the power given them by virtue of the wizardry of current digital technologies, they will redefine institutions without mercy. But higher education in the virtual world must guard against falling prey to standardless learning practices.

Another key driver, of course, is the interest of the money men or money women in this new economic good called education. Education is truly a renewable resource; attention to it will pay forever. Yet education is also a very complex enterprise; deep human emotions are involved. It is not an easy business, in the long haul. Incomplete understanding of this reality is most surely an obstacle. It is easy to pick off the sweet fruit, but the bitter needs to be nurtured too. Will business ever convince the public sector to give up half of the basket (and the most profitable half, at that)?

Traditional learning providers are in a bit of a quandary as well. For the moment, they still hold on to a considerable piece of property: knowledge workers (aka faculty), credentials (aka gate openers), culturally inculcated deference (aka faith in the established institutional order). So for now these institutions can help drive the LMS agenda. Before long however, all but the strongest traditional institutions and the most adaptive will bite the dust. Private companies will buy the research Ph.D.s., and the teaching will fall to others. So perhaps the major obstacle is the difficulty for every player to envision a future where it can still win.

Timing

Unless it lacks the strength and vision to define an authentic partnership—business, provider, learner—to the benefit of all, an institution should not wait to embark on an LMS partnership. Institutions that demur will disappear.

Leadership

Types of leaders needed for partnering in the learning marketspace include

- *Student leaders*—the impassioned voices of youth (not the cynical, pre–"real political career" types).

- *Academic leaders*—the nonhypocritical defenders of standards of learning. Without them, Western culture will sink in a morass of materialistic hedonism.

- *Community business leaders*—with an emphasis on community and on business. We normally think about business leaders in terms of a CEO of a multinational corporation. The job security of this individual depends on only one thing: growth in company stock to satisfy the stockholders. Some are very wise and sophisticated people indeed. Yet they cannot be trusted to betray their self-interest.

The evolution of the LMS partnership depends on multifaceted leaders, each in their own straitjacket and focused on only one concept: learning equals personal advancement, growth, and productivity, which equals employer satisfaction, which equals social and cultural benefit, which equals more investment in learning. This agenda requires putting a premium on the visionary, whether found among providers, customers, or employers.

JAAP TUINMAN is president and CEO of the Open Learning Agency, headquartered in Burnaby, British Columbia, Canada. The mission of the Open Learning Agency is to enhance the personal growth of individuals and their performance in society and in the workplace by providing high-quality, flexible learning products, services, and systems.

3

Priorities in a Learning Marketspace

Partnering in a learning marketspace does more than open new markets; it completely reshapes the nature and organization of higher education. The new priority is to enhance what we do—to transform learning through new forms of service, responsiveness, innovation, and partnership.

Preliminaries: Value Web Versus Value Chain

Unlike a physical or place-based partnership, which limits interaction to a fixed number of people or organizations, a partnership in a learning marketspace holds unlimited dimensions. According to Kelly (1998), "in the marketspace of networks, value flows in webs" (p. 97). To appreciate the importance of this development, we must draw a distinction between value chains and value webs, two contrasting models for understanding how value is added or enhanced in a collaborative process or undertaking.

A *value chain* is a linear mode of comprehending that one organization or operation adds value and passes that enhancement "downstream" to the next participant in the value-added process. NetAcademy, at the Institute for Media and Communications Management in St. Gallen, Switzerland, identifies the primary activities characterizing the value chain as inbound logistics, operations, outbound logistics, marketing and sales, and service, and along the way, such secondary activities as procurement, technology development, human resources, and the infrastructure of the organization (www.businessmedia.org/netacademy/glossary.nsf/KW_id_all/509). The process is the familiar one of the assembly line.

By contrast, a *value web* is a new paradigm in which the new realities of smaller organizations, virtual institutions, and complex interorganizational structures redefine how value is added by each participant in a process. "A new business model is emerging," writes Dorian Selz (1999) of NetAcademy. "Electronic networks and markets allow the breakup of [value chains or systems] previously thought to be firmly controlled . . . the value chain loses its chain attributes, and is replaced by a web of fluid and flexible relations. . . ."

Instead of partnering to carve out or preserve a niche in a value *chain*, the institution of higher education must partner to participate in a value *web*. As Sohail Inayatullah and Jennifer Gidley (2000) state, "The issue is not that the public intellectual has disappeared but that new spaces for action and reflection have been created" (p. 5).

A Continuum of Prioritizing

Partnership is especially difficult because the priorities of those involved in establishing it—as well as the cultures of the corresponding institutions—may differ considerably.

Comments from our initial interviews with those involved in an interinstitutional partnership illustrated this continuum of priorities and, in some cases, a propensity to want to control the value chain as opposed to participating in a value web—for example, one university administrator saw the partnership as potentially getting in the way of improving the competitiveness of his own institution. Another college executive saw it as a way to increase access to the underprivileged, while a businessperson in a major corporation was most concerned about scalability. Others thought the partnership should be used to strengthen what already existed on the physical campus or saw it as an opportunity to enhance learning capacity and the ongoing access to learning.

As these reactions illustrate, the impact of a partnership on an institution depends on its values and priorities. An institution intent on controlling a partnership is not a valid partner. An institution that views partnership as a means to enhance access and the pedagogy of learning has an elevating priority and gives the partnership the potential to have a positive impact on the institution.

Furthermore, note the contrast between the perspectives we have just summarized and how business and industry typically view partnership. Kelly (1998) states that "established firms are . . . weaving dozens, if not hundreds, of alliances and partnerships; seeking out as many networks of affiliation and common cause as possible, sharing the risk by making a web. A motley caravan of firms can cross a suboptimal stretch with hope. Banding together . . . allows knowledge about the terrain to be shared" (p. 92).

Businesses clearly have partnered, merged, or been taken over as a consequence of the existing business climate. If we view education from this e-commerce perspective, we can say that the sphere of influence is now global instead of geographically specific, thanks to the capacity of technology, societal demands, and the learner's sophistication and expectations.

Rethinking Competition

In digital-age business, it is said that your partner should be your competitor. In higher education, our competition used to be institutions in geographic proximity or some similar niche; we were in competition for a limited number of place-bound students. In a space-based environment, though, can any one institution become a comprehensive deliverer of educational services, programming, certification, and degrees in this context of lifelong learning and mass customization?

We would say no. No one institution has enough human, intellectual, and fiscal infrastructure to meet the complex needs and services that exist in an e-environment. Hence, MIT partners with

Microsoft, Hungry Minds allies with Yahoo!, Columbia University and others found Fathom.com, and so on.

So, why should higher education institutions partner—with each other or with dot coms?

For many, not partnering means bringing on the eventual demise of the institution. But is that really going to happen to, for example, a major land-grant research university in the United States? Can any institution be an entity either within its own niche or in a geographic sense and yet evolve slowly into an online, on-site entity without partners? Is a one-stop institution-centric portal enough for what society demands of an educational institution? As Inayatullah and Gidley (2000) state, "If elite institutions do not follow this path [toward virtual space and partnerships], believing that they will retain their market share irrespective of virtualization and the impacts of globalization, new low-cost players like the convenience-oriented University of Phoenix or rich mammoth multimedia players like News Corporation and Disney will step in" (p. 5). Or, as John Fry, executive vice president of the University of Pennsylvania, says, "Rather than *being* lunch, Penn will *do* lunch with prospective partners" (as quoted by Grills, 2000; italics added).

Five Specific Priorities in Partnering in the Learning Marketspace

Our thesis, then, is not to partner with just any organization. An organization should partner as a means to empower learners and enhance its mission. In this section we offer five areas in which your institution might begin a discussion specifically about priorities for partnering in the learning marketspace. Keep in mind that (1) these are priorities for partnering in virtual space, not a physical place, (2) any partnership attempting to build a learning marketspace must be aware that it is dealing with a winner-take-all environment (see Chapter Two), and (3) the hallmark of a learning marketspace is its emphasis on learner control and relationship building (see Chapter Five).

Cultural Shift in Learning

The first priority is to understand that only through partnership can an institution expand educational capacity to the point being expected, and increasingly demanded, by learners. Here the goals should be to

- Enhance access and the pedagogy of learning as well as improve learning regardless of learner location

- Put the learner in charge—that is, develop the tools and pedagogy to help the learner make the cultural shift from attending a lecture to managing knowledge (see Chapter Five, specifically the e-portfolio concept)

Participation in a Global Economy

Second, a global economy requires educational restructuring. Learners and industries no longer tolerate delay; they expect partnership, access, and response to their needs. Thus, organizations should partner in order to

- Build new economic, intellectual, and social capital to meet the needs of a global economy

- Provide an opportunity to participate in the global higher education enterprise and economy

Standardization and Scalability

Kelly (1998) writes that "eventually technical standards will become as important as laws. . . . As networks mature, and make the transition from ad hoc prestandard free-for-alls to fluid hot spots of innovation, and then into full-fledged systems with deeply embedded standards, standards increasingly ossify into something like laws" (p. 71). Standardization doesn't mean that everyone does the same thing; nor does it mean that all higher education institutions should look the same. It means that learners who are increasingly taking advantage of the multiple opportunities of e-space should no longer be expected to decipher the idiosyncratic system of each institution.

Thus, from the viewpoint of the third priority (scalability), standardization means that we partner to "minimize capital costs, reduce operating costs, and maximize geographic reach" (Grills, 2000). In other words, we should

- Capitalize on the strengths of the partner(s) and restructure our institution to take advantage of partnership

---

The IMS Global Learning Consortium

The important area of online learning scalability and technology standards for higher education and lifelong learning resources is the interest of the IMS Global Learning Consortium, Inc. IMS defines and delivers interoperable, XML-based specifications for exchanging learning content and moving information among learning system components. IMS members are implementing products and adopting these specifications in programs in order to make online learning easier and cheaper to deliver anywhere and anytime. They are also creating new learning mechanisms, new contexts for learning, and new products for education and training providers.

IMS originated as a project of the EDUCAUSE National Learning Infrastructure Initiative (NLII). In late 1999, it became a separate nonprofit corporation. More than 250 organizations have already joined IMS in order to participate in meeting its collective objectives. These members include hardware and software vendors, publishers, Web service providers, e-commerce companies, educational institutions,

- Create shared infrastructures, for example, a common information technology infrastructure or mutually beneficial professional development opportunities

Net-Centric Niche

The fourth priority for partnership should be less to entrench one's niche and more to design and enable access to aggregated learning opportunities (or a "net-centric" niche). An institution's niche may no longer exist in the learning marketspace. Again, according to Kelly, "Rich, interactive, and highly flexible in shape, the network economy resembles a biome seething with action, a jungle in fast-forward motion. New niches open up constantly and vanish quickly. Competitors sprout beneath you and then gobble your spot up. One day you are king of the mountain, and the next day there is no

---

government agencies, network providers, systems integrators, multimedia content providers, and other consortia. Representation from almost all of the constituencies involved in online learning, as well as active collaboration with related specifications and standards organizations, enables IMS to provide a neutral forum for balancing the competing business interests and different decision-making objectives behind real-world use of online learning.

IMS is developing and promoting open specifications for locating and using educational content, tracking learner capacities and progress, reporting learner performance, and exchanging course records between administrative systems. The initial IMS specifications already are becoming worldwide de facto standards for defining acquisition requirements and for delivering learning products and services. Cooperation with other organizations to promote the use of IMS and other specifications encourages their accreditation by international standards bodies.

mountain at all" (1998, p. 83). An institution should avoid cling-
ing to a niche area in the learning marketspace; instead, it should

- Take advantage of the unlimited dimensions of a
  network space

- Study its assets in relation to a value web instead of a
  linear value chain

- Work to bring to market, through partnership, a very
  different value proposition from what is available

Human Relationships

Information looms everywhere and grows exponentially in the
learning marketspace. To add value to this information, the fifth

IMS SPECIFICATION LIST	
IMS Specification	*What the Specification Covers*
Meta-data v1.0, v1.1	Attributes to describe learning resources
Enterprise Interworking v1.0, v1.1	Formats for exchanging student and course information between system components
Content Packaging v1.0	Instructions for wrapping and exchanging learning content
Question and Test Interoperability v1.0	Formats for constructing and exchanging assessment information
Under development:	
Content Management	Specifications for the behavior of content at run time
Learner Information Packaging and Exchange	Information about learners
Instructional Design	Definitions of learning scenarios and interactions
Accessibility	Specifications for use by disabled and disadvantaged learners

priority is to focus on human relationships. Partnering to create a learning marketspace begins with and is sustained by human relationships. Only through communicating and developing strong relationships can institutions partner to

- Respond quickly in meeting the needs of lifelong learners

- Engage learners with the higher education enterprise

- Share risks while working toward mass customization

The priorities of partnering in a learning marketspace then revolve around the learner as well as the new opportunities and exigencies opening up in electronic spaces. For the learner, the

---

IMS working groups have two key goals: (1) defining the technical specifications for interoperability of applications and services in distributed learning, and (2) supporting widespread adoption of specifications into products and services and into programs and projects worldwide. The working groups gather functional requirements, technical capabilities, and deployment priorities from end users, vendors, purchasers, policymakers, and program planners. These inputs are consolidated into one or more specifications as the groups produce and critique a specification package consisting of a definition, binding, and best practice guide.

A technical board on which every member is represented reviews working group products in detail before drafts or formal releases are made available to the public via the IMS Web site (www.imsproject.org). Released specifications are made available to the public without charge, and feedback from test beds, product developers, and adopters is incorporated through systematic revision cycles.

EDWARD C. T. WALKER
Chief Executive Officer
IMS Global Learning Consortium

digital age requires new ways of developing, managing, and sharing knowledge in a lifelong learning context. This calls for new technologies, learning relationships, and pedagogies, which can only be developed and maintained if an institution leverages resources through partnership. The same is true of the need for scalable services, which learners increasingly demand as they move from institution to institution to select the opportunities that best meet their learning needs.

At the same time, with their unlimited connections, links, relationships, and capacity for aggregation of content and services, e-spaces offer new opportunities to meet the needs of these new learners. Yet e-spaces also redefine how business is done, notably in the shift from value chain to value web and the emergence of new opportunities for competition and partnering.

Overall, once we move beyond an institution-centric focus, the priorities for partnering are compelling. In the remainder of this chapter, we focus on what we see as the most critical among these priorities: economic development and our social contract.

The Priority of Economic Development and the Social Contract

An institution should engage in a partnership as a means of attending to the needs of lifelong learners. Even so, this admonishment is not always persuasive, in part because learning is but one of the missions attended to by many of our institutions. The more compelling argument is that, at its core, partnering is about rural, state, regional, national, and international development of economic, intellectual, and social capital. It is about responsibility, about our institutional contract with society.

As one example of this responsibility, between 1996 and 2006, the state of Minnesota will have to fill five hundred thousand new jobs that require postsecondary training or education. The city of

Rochester, home to IBM and the Mayo Clinic, will experience a short-age of twenty-four thousand skilled workers within the next decade.

Meanwhile, small towns on the Iron Range of northern Minn-esota are losing the economic development battle: companies hes-itate to locate in the region or are moving out because they cannot find enough skilled workers, and young people are migrating to the cities to find educational and economic opportunities. A 1998 Blandin Foundation report stated that "Minnesota's low jobless rate *illustrates what could be the national trend: a shortage of skilled workers.* As unemployment nationwide dips, Minnesota's plight is emerging as an important test case. In order to keep growing, Minnesota must find creative ways to attract new workers—and increase the pro-ductivity of current employees" (p. 10, italics added).

Consider the exigency in the second half of the nineteenth cen-tury: growing need for more highly trained professionals; a society frustrated with a largely unresponsive set of higher education insti-tutions; and concern that the unlimited opportunities of the Amer-ican dream were being threatened by industrialization (Bonnen, 1998). The nation's response to these needs was to create a new kind of college or university: the land-grant institution, dedicated to "(1) educating and training the professional cadres of an indus-trial, increasingly urban, society; (2) providing broad access to high education, irrespective of wealth or social status; and (3) working to improve the welfare and social status of the largest, then most disadvantaged, groups in society" (p. 29).

Consider the similarities today: growing need nationally and internationally for more skilled professionals, especially in infor-mation technology professions; a society frustrated with a seemingly unresponsive set of higher education institutions; and intense concern—articulated as the "digital divide"—for those most threat-ened by the information age. The land-grant institutions of today have responded to these needs by issuing a call to become "engaged" institutions.

A Call for Engagement and Commitment to the Social Contract

Twenty-four college and university presidents, in a 1999 Kellogg Commission report titled *Returning to Our Roots: A Learning Society*, declared that to create a learning society, education should be accessible and promoted to people of all ages. In the vision of this commission, an engaged institution responds to the needs of its current students and tomorrow's, not yesterday's. An engaged institution stimulates and organizes exchange, in partnership with learning communities organized by interest and geography. The report suggests that universities partner with elementary and secondary schools, businesses, and governments to increase access to and development of lifelong learning resources. In short, the commission calls upon us to

1. Make lifelong learning a part of our core public mission. This means to increase and promote access, partnerships, mission differentiation, and accreditation across systems.

2. Create new kinds of learning environments that promote higher-order reasoning abilities, upgrading skills, faculty development, research on learning, and the use of technology in teaching.

3. Provide public support for lifelong learning through public investment, research, infrastructure support, and new financial aid policies.

However, the stark reality is that currently, with a few exceptions, the majority of land-grant institutions in the United States are not leading the effort to develop a twenty-first century "outreach" university in the sense of meeting the needs of lifelong learners. Instead, other types of university, one being the mega-university, have forged innovative paths toward engaging learners.

The Mega-University and the Social Contract

Sir John Daniel, vice-chancellor of the Open University in the United Kingdom and now also president of the U.S. Open University, says that "the most important innovation in higher education in the last fifty years has been the creation and growth of the large distance teaching universities which I call *mega-universities*" (1999a). Though this development benefits small organizations, mega-universities are huge. Mega-universities are those having more than one hundred thousand learners, designed in large part to address the needs of a knowledge-age society; provide broad access to higher education, irrespective of wealth or social status; and improve the welfare and social status of disadvantaged groups in society. In short, their priorities are access, cost, and quality.

Already-aging data from 1996 illustrate the enormous "cost revolution" occurring with the introduction of eleven mega-universities worldwide (Table 3.1).

The priority that has allowed these mega-universities to meet twenty-first century challenges is summed up by Daniel (1999a) as the "soft technologies" or the "processes, approaches, sets of rules and models of organisation" that underpin today's global economy. The four key ingredients are "excellent learning materials; individual academic support to each student; effective administration and logistics; and teaching rooted in research."

Table 3.1. Cost Revolution at Mega-Universities

	Number of Colleges and Universities	Total Enrollment	Total Cost Per Year	Average Spent Per Student
United States	3,500	14.0 million	$175 billion	$12,500
Great Britain	182	1.6 million	$16 billion	$10,000
Mega-universities	11	2.8 million	$1 billion	$350

Source: Daniel, 1999a.

The Open University has partnered with Florida State University and California State University to produce programs that address challenges of cost, access, and quality through a teamwork model. According to Daniel, "there was at first deep skepticism but it was followed remarkably quickly by the zeal of conversion" (1999a). The courses and programs developed together become part of the partnership's learning marketspace. They have a life independent of the individual faculty members or individual institutions contributing to the development, and the focus is on the learner. We commend Florida State and California State for the courage and vision to partner on behalf of the learner.

The need for intellectual and social capital in our society clearly is immense. According to Robert Putnam (1995), Dillon Professor of International Affairs at Harvard University, "By analogy with notions of physical and human capital—tools and training that enhance individual productivity—'social capital' refers to features of a social organization such as networks, norms, and social trust that facilitate coordination and cooperation for mutual benefit. . . . Social connections and civic engagement pervasively influence our public life, as well as our private prospects" (p. 4).

Of interest, then, is the fact that, after having used distance study, 46 percent of graduates of the Open University report enhanced interest in current affairs, 40 percent become more interested in helping people in need, 20 percent become more involved in cultural activities, and 10 percent become more involved in political activities. These percentages represent a significantly greater number of learners "engaged" with their communities and with society than those graduating from mainstream institutions (Daniel, 1999b).

We cannot afford to miss the opportunity for people to realize their potential by allowing some learners to remain disenfranchised. Advances in communication, collaboration, and distance education have shown that we have the ability to teach virtually any learner. But doing so requires both institutional and individual commitment to using technology and assuming new roles; supporting programs and faculty as they learn new skills and revise courses, thus creating a ubiquitous infrastructure; and revising policies.

These issues cannot be addressed in institutional isolation. Because of the magnitude of the need and the immediacy of the problem, strategic coalition and partnership is imperative. Higher education cannot view itself, nor allow others to view it, as separate, distinct, or segregated from its social contract with society. We need to work together to develop partnerships and their accompanying portals to ensure access and equity as well as control of the process by lifelong learners.

Metro Alliance

We conclude this section on economic development and the social contract by describing a partnership designed to address the needs of underprepared and underserved learners in the Minneapolis–St. Paul metropolitan area. Ten technical and community colleges and a state university have developed the Metro Alliance. The vision is to be a high-quality, integrated, higher education system that functions like a single institution from the vantage point of the learners.

The Metro Alliance envisions a future in which learners move freely into and among the eleven member institutions. Compatible curricula, registration, and other key services allow students to take advantage of the array of programs offered at various times and locations throughout the Twin Cities metropolitan area. A learner might pursue a single degree by taking general education classes during lunch at a campus near work, while pursuing classes toward the major in the evening nearer-home or via the Internet.

The mission states that "the Metro Alliance unites eleven distinct MnSCU [Minnesota State Colleges and Universities] institutions to better prepare the diverse residents of the Twin Cities metropolitan area for learning, employment, citizenship, and life. The Alliance provides seamless pathways for students at all levels of educational achievement and strengthens member institutions, both individually and collectively" (*Crosstown Connections*, 1999, p. 3). The partnership serves wide-ranging learners from all over the metropolitan area and helps them achieve their various learning goals. Learners are able to walk into any Alliance institution and match interests and skills with Alliance services, courses, and programs that help them achieve their goals.

To meet the needs of underprepared and underserved learners, the Alliance works with high schools and other key groups to ensure that the institutions have a clear understanding of learners' post-secondary educational options as well as clear processes to enroll in higher education institutions that meet their learning needs and goals. The Alliance also works with community leaders and community-based organizations to identify and meet the learning needs and goals of underserved learners. They work with minority communities to help colleges create a culturally sensitive atmosphere and high-quality services and programs to meet the learning needs and styles of diverse populations.

The first goal of the partnering organizations is to give learners enrolled at each Alliance institution access to programs and services offered by any other Alliance institution. The outcomes include

- Complete articulation of courses between similar programs at Alliance institutions.

- No unnecessary course/program duplication in new and existing undergraduate and graduate programs at Metro Alliance institutions.

- Students can use course equivalencies, academic program information, transfer course evaluations, and degree audits in a Web-based environment through the full implementation of the . . . Course Applicability System (CAS).

- Students have access to compatible admission, registration, financial aid, transcript, scheduling, and other services for all Metro Alliance institutions at each Alliance institution.
- Students . . . have access to specialty programs offered by Alliance institutions.
- Other MnSCU institutions coordinate the courses and programs they offer in the metropolitan area through the Metro Alliance. [*Crosstown Connections*, 1999, p. 12]

Their second goal is to increase enrollment. Here the strategies include

- Working with educational, business, and community leaders from the communities of color in the metropolitan area
- Reviewing and collaborating with current initiatives like the Minnesota Minority Education Partnership counseling study
- Working with K–12 initiatives such as "Bridge" programs to develop relationships with elementary and secondary students of color and their parents and help them to plan and prepare for their educational future
- Working with community outreach and high school guidance counselors to review and improve the processes used to prepare young people of color to choose and enroll in a college
- Creating and funding visible support networks, liaisons, and affinity groups for students of color to increase their positive experiences in each Alliance institution

- Creating and funding recruitment and retention processes for each Alliance institution to attract more students from protected class groups

- Assisting in the development of scholarship funds, mentoring programs, and other support for protected class groups and first-generation college students [*Crosstown Connections*, 1999, pp. 15–16]

When institutions decide to partner to improve learning access and outcomes, the impact on the learner is great. The future of our institutions and our society depends upon how well we partner in the learning marketspace.

References

Blandin Foundation Task Force on Worker Training. *Worker Education in Greater Minnesota: The Need for Lifelong Learning.* Report. Grand Rapids, Minn.: Blandin Foundation, 1998.

Bonnen, J. T. "The Land-Grant Idea and the Evolving Outreach University." In R. M. Lerner and L.A.K. Simon (eds.), *University-Community Collaborations for the Twenty-First Century: Outreach to Scholarship for Youth and Families.* New York: Garland, 1998.

Crosstown Connections: Academic Plan for the Twin Cities Metropolitan Area. Minnesota State Colleges and Universities. Nov. 1999.

Daniel, J. "Innovation at Scale in the Delivery of Learning and Teaching: Will the Whole Be Greater than the Sum of the Parts?" Presentation to the Twelfth International Meeting of University Administrators, Sept. 6, 1999a. [www.open.ac.uk./vcs-speeches/edin-admin.htm].

Daniel, J. "Lifelong Learning for an Ignorant World." Presentation to National Association of State Universities and Land Grant Colleges, San Francisco, Nov. 8, 1999b. [www.open.ac.uk/vcs-speeches/NASULGC.htm].

Grills, C. M. "Lead or Bleed: Colleges, Universities and the E-Universe." *Business Officer,* Apr. 2000. [www.nacubo.org/website/members/bomag/00/04/bleed.html].

Inayatullah, S., and Gidley, J. "Trends Transforming the Universities of This Century: Virtualize, Disappear, or Transform." *On the Horizon,* 2000, 8(2), 1–6.

Kellogg Commission on the Future of State and Land-Grant Universities. *Returning to Our Roots: A Learning Society*. Report for National Association of State Universities and Land-Grant Colleges, 1999. [www.nasulgc.org/publications/Kellogg/Learn.pdf].

Kelly, K. *New Rules for the New Economy: 10 Radical Strategies for a Connected World*. New York: Penguin, 1998.

Putnam, R. D. "Bowling Alone: America's Declining Social Capital." *Current*, 1995, *373*, 3–9.

Selz, D. "Value Webs: Emerging Forms of Fluid and Flexible Organizations." Dissertation, University of St. Gallen, Switzerland, 1999. [www.businessmedia.org/netacademy/publications.nsf/all_pk/1305].

Perspective: Sir John Daniel and Robin Mason

In our view, the best—or at least the smoothest-running—learning marketspace partnerships are those between complementary institutions, rather than between similar ones. In the UK Open University (OU), for example, we have a longstanding relationship with the British Broadcasting Corporation in which our content expertise and their production skills can be married in the search for outstanding visual learning material.

A much more recent partnership for us is with Research Machines, in a government-funded project to provide IT training for school teachers throughout Britain. We contribute the teaching and they contribute the machines, the access, and a whole range of contacts, which have benefited the project enormously.

Finally, we have a partnership with the College of Law to provide law courses to students at a distance. In this case, our partner has the content and we have the distance education expertise.

Partnerships of this kind, where each provides what the other needs but does not have, are much easier to form and operate than those between or among similar institutions, where petty jealousies; institutional defense mechanisms; and other fears about loss of autonomy, reputation, or influence frequently arise. Furthermore, there are often tangible barriers, such as different timetables, curricula, and pedagogies, all of which are real hurdles to partnering for similar institutions.

Another type of partnership that the OU and other institutions have carried out successfully for a long time is what might be called institution building, usually in developing countries. As the developing partner grows local expertise in preparing and delivering its own courses, the partnership becomes less and less necessary and is eventually terminated.

Influence on Education

There are many views on the question of how these partnerships will influence education and educational delivery systems.

The Luddite view is that the new providers in the new marketspaces are merely cherry-picking the low-hanging fruit: well-educated, upwardly mobile learners with good access to technology who are keen to improve their employability. Universities will be left with the eighteen-to-twenty-two-year-old market and all those who want a good degree and recognizable qualifications.

Those who believe we are facing a paradigm shift talk volubly about the death of the university, about a client-centered marketplace in which the curriculum, the providers, and the delivery methodologies will be quite different. Getting into the right partnerships now is the only way of surviving.

Finally, there is a middle ground: the gradual, evolutionary model in which existing providers jockey for position alongside new providers and new partnerships, the competition increases, some closures take place, and eventually we all realize there have been major changes in our thinking about teaching and learning.

We subscribe to the evolutionary model. At the OU we strive to lead the way in changing our organization, our thinking, our delivery system, our partners, and our curriculum to meet the needs of the changing marketspace.

Driving Forces and Obstacles

The driving forces for the rise of partnership among educational providers are the opportunities for reaching new markets; for offering more choice, flexibility, and access; and for capitalizing on the development of new technologies. In the case of the OU's partnership with the College of Law, we knew from our market surveying that our students most wanted us to offer law courses and qualifications. Seeking a partner was the speediest and most economical way of meeting their demands.

The biggest obstacle to successful partnering is the need for each side to come to terms with the other partner, who is inevitably marching to a different drum. For example, one partner may be seeking to reach a wide, popular audience, while the other is concerned about quality and standards.

It is also problematic when either partner is unsure about its mission or is new and unformed as an institution. This is rather the case in the much-publicized U.S. Open University/Western Governors University partnership. Both parties are still trying to establish themselves, and trying to partner under such circumstances is like trying to hit a moving target.

Timing

In terms of when it is appropriate to form a partnership, it follows that an organization needs a strong vision of where it is heading and what market it is hoping to capture. This helps to steer through the current variety of opportunities to form a partnership. Much time and energy can be consumed in discussion and early negotiation with potential partners if the leadership is not clear about its aims and the gaps in its current ability to fulfill the aims.

Leadership

The old form of a gentlemen's agreement upon which some institutions still rely is not going to be dynamic enough for the fast-paced, complex, and demanding environment that the learning marketspace has become. Strategic thinking is needed from leaders, but understanding learning, today's learner, and the learning environment is necessary for the grounding that allows one to keep a steady eye on the ultimate target.

SIR JOHN DANIEL is vice chancellor of the United Kingdom Open University.

ROBIN MASON is a professor and director of the master's program in open and distance education at the United Kingdom Open University.

4

Assessing Readiness for Partnerships

Initially, an LMS partnership might appear foolish, since it may at first underperform existing institutions with regard to the criteria of the traditional mainstream market. The reality of the twenty-first century, however, indicates otherwise. Learners expect seamless, lifelong, affordable, asynchronous, interactive, diverse, customized, specialized, learner-centered higher education. They expect us to partner in delivering the learning resources they need. A Minnesota state planning report (Minnesota Planning, 1998, p. 7) represents the sentiments of our citizens: "If Minnesota's higher education institutions—both public and private—are to thrive . . . they need to see themselves as brokers of educational services, rather than as competitors fighting for enrollment and public funds, and they need to work cooperatively to provide affordable services."

Local constituents may expect us to partner, but the global economy demands it. According to Thomas Friedman (1999), a handful of rules govern this new economy, including the following:

- Shrink the size of the bureaucracy.

- Eliminate and lower tariffs on imported goods.

- Remove restrictions on foreign investment.

- Get rid of quotas and domestic monopolies.

- Increase exports.

- Make currency convertible.

- Promote domestic competition.

- Allow citizens to choose from an array of choices.

These rules argue that, as we look to developing a learning marketspace, any partnering institution should consider

- Developing one information technology structure and one lifelong learning organization

- Charging the same tuition for virtual learning resources regardless of where they originate

- Locating the best virtual learning resource to meet a citizen's need, going outside of the resource base of the partnership if need be

- Promoting its collective virtual learning resources to the world's learning marketplace

- Making credits transferable among all partners

- Allowing citizens to choose from an array of offerings

However persuasive or stringent the demands of a global economy, the majority of colleges and universities respond largely by continuing to pour millions into internal systems rather than partnering to leverage resources. Given that one's partners no longer need be determined by geography, this reluctance to partner is even more astounding. As Michael Beller and Ehud Or (1998) note, large leading universities can perhaps get by using their own resources to develop the necessary information technology systems needed in the digital age, but "unfortunately, since universities generally wish to preserve their autonomy, the establishment of such coalitions is rather unlikely. Bridging the gap between the reality of stand-alone operations and the need for pooling resources will turn out to be a challenge in and of itself."

Assessing Readiness for a Higher Education Partnership

The challenge in partnering is great. The means to get there begin with assessing readiness. In his comparative case study of eight organizations from higher education, industry, and state governments involved in developing virtual universities, Scott Rosevear (1999) developed five questions intended to help assess readiness: "What is the state's technological infrastructure? How prepared are the traditional colleges and universities to support virtual learning environments? Do they all have equal technological capabilities? What is a reasonable prediction for how long it will take before the virtual university is operational? What are the resource gaps, and how will they be filled?"

On the basis of our experience in partnership initiatives, we originally focused on eight criteria in determining readiness for partnering in the learning marketspace.

1. *Learner and faculty needs.* Are there learning opportunities otherwise denied by existing traditional institutions? Do faculty have the opportunity to offer their expertise innovatively to the citizens of the world?

2. *Leadership committed to the effort.* Is there support, both vertical and horizontal, across the institution and among systems? Is there significant buy-in from key stakeholders?

3. *E-commerce strategy.* Do the partners have an e-commerce strategy? Does this strategy emphasize lifelong learning (that is, innovative partnerships between education and industry)?

4. *International strategy.* Do the partners have an international strategy? Does it emphasize lifelong learning?

5. *Identification of "crucial" industries, and a clear economic development plan.* The Michigan Virtual Automotive and Manufacturing College was begun in large part to protect a crucial industry in the state. In the circumstances you face, have the partners identified crucial industries to preserve, protect, and foster?

6. *Climate to support partnership and change.* Are incentives in place to foster collaboration across systems?

7. *Resources.* Is there a minimum of $5 million committed to the initiative? Many learning marketspace initiatives have failed simply because they did not have the monetary resources to build and sustain such an effort.

8. *Commitment to learner-centered education.* So much has been written about the need for learner-centered systems that we hesitate to add this to our list. However, as noted earlier, most institutions focus first on what the partnership brings to them rather than on what it should bring to learners.

A Survey on Readiness

We found there was a need for a more comprehensive list of readiness criteria to help potential partners understand and identify those criteria that are of greatest importance. Therefore, we integrated our criteria with those of Rosevear into a survey (extracted in Exhibit 4.1). Naturally, any list of readiness criteria depends on the context and culture of the initiative. Nevertheless, the survey is intended as a way to focus initial partnership attention on whether or not the parties involved are indeed ready.

To date, we have asked four distinct groups to complete this survey:

Exhibit 4.1. Survey of Readiness Criteria for Establishing a Partnership

Please indicate in the right column the value you attribute to the following readiness criteria for establishing an academic e-partnership.

Not = Not important
Less = Less important
Imp = Important
Extr = Extremely important

Using the blanks to the left of the items, please indicate your top three criteria. (Number them 1, 2, and 3.)

_____	Technological infrastructure of the state	Not	Less	Imp	Extr
_____	Technological infrastructure of the individual colleges and institutions	Not	Less	Imp	Extr
_____	Level of equality among the institutions in terms of technological infrastructure	Not	Less	Imp	Extr
_____	Reasonable time (five years) to become operational	Not	Less	Imp	Extr
_____	Identification of resource gaps and a strategy for filling them	Not	Less	Imp	Extr
_____	Public funding (e.g., from the legislature)	Not	Less	Imp	Extr
_____	Private funding (e.g., from corporations)	Not	Less	Imp	Extr
_____	Establishment of public-private partnerships	Not	Less	Imp	Extr
_____	Leadership committed to the effort	Not	Less	Imp	Extr
_____	Buy-in by faculty/departments/colleges	Not	Less	Imp	Extr
_____	A state e-commerce strategy	Not	Less	Imp	Extr
_____	A state strategy for international work	Not	Less	Imp	Extr
_____	Identification of crucial industries to foster	Not	Less	Imp	Extr
_____	Climate to support partnership and change	Not	Less	Imp	Extr
_____	Commitment to learner-centered education	Not	Less	Imp	Extr
_____	Strategic integration of K–12 and higher education goals	Not	Less	Imp	Extr
_____	Alignment of key decision makers	Not	Less	Imp	Extr
_____	Other: _____	Not	Less	Imp	Extr

- Those attending the presentation of a paper on institutional readiness for partnership efforts, at the 1999 EDUCAUSE annual conference. Twenty-two attendees volunteered to complete the survey, with the greatest number of respondents being administrators from four-year graduate institutions ($N = 7$) or system offices ($N = 8$).

- A nearly equal mix of higher education and K–12 faculty attending a Minnesota Workforce Conference ($N = 77$).

- A group of agricultural economics department heads attending a national workshop on partnering in distance education ($N = 19$), all from four-year graduate land-grant institutions.

- A group of CEOs representing virtual university efforts from around the world ($N = 8$).

The READY Project

The National Learning Infrastructure Initiative (NLII, www.educause.edu/nlii) is an EDUCAUSE program dedicated to harnessing the power of information technology to improve the quality of teaching and learning, contain or reduce costs, and provide better access to American higher education.

The NLII is a sponsor of the READY (READiness inventorY) project, which includes the development of a Web-based decision tool (see www.educause.edu/ready) organized around the concept of institutional readiness for any number of transformative goals. The tool will have two parts: the engine, which is content-neutral, making it flexible enough to handle many types of decisions; and the content itself, which will provide a conceptual framework for a particular decision, identifying the issues and critical success factors.

Those attending the EDUCAUSE presentation indicated these five criteria to be of greatest importance (listed from highest to lowest) in terms of readiness for partnership:

1. Leadership committed to the effort
2. Commitment to learner-centered education
3. Climate to support partnership and change
4. Alignment of key decision makers
5. Buy-in by faculty/departments/colleges

Although a distinctly different audience, those attending the Minnesota conference indicated exactly the same five criteria to be of greatest importance to them, with "leadership committed to the change" and "commitment to learner-centered education" again being the top two choices.

The agricultural economics department heads also chose leadership commitment as their top criterion, followed by faculty/

By guiding users interactively through a series of considerations, the READY tool will help an institution understand its current situation, promote a constructive and respectful dialogue, and support the development of a meaningful and effective strategic plan. As research, case studies, and other materials for a particular content area become available, the tool can also ultimately serve as a diagnostic and inventory tool. Both the process and the results of the self-assessment will empower an institution to apply scarce resources strategically, address weaknesses, take advantage of strengths, and move the institution further along the transformation continuum, whether it is to move to an emphasis on learner-centered teaching or to develop effective interinstitutional partnerships.

department/college buy-in, technological infrastructure, supportive climate, and a reasonable time to become operational.

The virtual university CEOs also listed leadership commitment and buy-in among their top choices, but they placed great importance on "identification of crucial industries to foster" as well.

Although these groups represent small sample sizes (whose results therefore cannot be generalized), they nonetheless indicate a consensus across these different groups: to be ready for a partnership initiative, you need—above all else—leadership committed to the effort, commitment to learner-centered education, a climate to support partnership and change, and buy-in.

Robinson and Daigle's Conceptual Framework

In their thorough analysis of California State University's failed partnership (known as the California Educational Technology Initiative, or CETI), Maynard Robinson and Stephen Daigle conclude that

> A desire to increase institutional resources and conduct business differently is necessary but not enough to form a partnership. Partnership preparation requires careful self-examination or a readiness assessment before engaging in a partnership. Such a readiness assessment can serve two purposes. The first is to help determine whether a university lends itself to a partnership arrangement; that is, if it can accommodate itself to such a formal relationship. The second is to promote a process of shared ownership: to identify those areas in which a university must be prepared to alter current organizational arrangements or patterns of behavior to increase the likelihood of forming a successful partnership. The readiness assessment will be worthwhile only if it takes into account the contextual

elements of the university, its public status, and its social and political characteristics. [1999–2000, p. 19]

Drawing on public management theory, Robinson and Daigle present a conceptual framework for gauging readiness for public-private partnership development. Their framework integrates an action context (descriptive-explanatory, normative, assumptive, and instrumental actions) with a developmental sequence (vision → commitment → culture → risk → power → adaptability). In Table 4.1 we present a synthesis of their framework, creating a series of steps and a corresponding set of framing questions as an initial blueprint for partnering in the learning marketspace.

Robinson and Daigle note that each partner usually begins by asking, "How will it work, and what are the consequences for me?" (1999–2000, p. 21). We have found that, given the likely complexity of such affairs in the twenty-first century, successful partners are generally going to be those who are willing to engage with one another amid a significant level of ambiguity. Lessons learned from the California CETI partnership include the need to "communicate early and often," recognition that "partnership formulation is a process of discovery and disclosure," and knowing that partnership formation should "be fluid, with the capacity to replace partners if a suitable match cannot be made" (p. 29).

The authors conclude by saying that the CETI partnership should have started small and worked toward building a relationship incrementally, rather than articulating a grand vision or ambition and then working backward toward more realistic and manageable goals. Indeed, the fate of CETI is hauntingly similar to that of California Virtual University, another initiative that started with a grandiose vision that had to be scaled back mere months after it began (in 1997).

Overall, commitment alone does not constitute readiness. Readiness "requires tolerance for undefined boundaries, unfamiliar

Table 4.1. An Initial Blueprint for Partnering in the Learning Marketspace

Step	Questions to Address
Description	What is the partnership? How will it affect my institution?
Beliefs	What are the guiding, foundational principles?
Assumptions	What can my institution assume that we can achieve together from this partnership? What will each partner do or be responsible for?
Operations	How will the partnership work? Is it feasible?
Vision	What is the greater vision or greater social good?
Commitment	Are multiple levels committed to the partnership? Are levels of trust and covenants in place?
Collaboration	Are collaboration and cooperation more important than hierarchy and competition?
Risk	Can we tolerate the financial, legal, academic, and experimentation risks?
Control	Who has the authority? Where are clear lines drawn?
Adaptation	Are we willing to alter the direction, structure, and operations to support the partnership?

Source: Adapted from Robinson and Daigle (1999–2000).

management practices and new authority relationships, and complex benefits that are sometimes hard to measure" (p. 30). In short, entering into a partnership is more than cooperating or collaborating: it is a melding of cultures, a merger of the unfamiliar, a new way of life.

Partnership formation is indeed a process of discovery and disclosure; readiness begins with establishing communication, trust, and support. If communication and trust are established, and if the leadership is willing to embrace the disruptive potential that the learning marketspace represents, then once birthed it is likely to be unstoppable.

References

Beller, M., and Or, E. "The Crossroads Between Lifelong Learning and Information Technology: A Challenge Facing Leading Universities." *Journal of Computer and Mediated Communication*, 1998, 4(2). [www.ascusc.org/jcmc/vol4/issue2/beller.html].

Friedman, T. *The Lexus and the Olive Tree*. New York: Farrar, Straus & Giroux, 1999.

Minnesota Planning. *Balancing the Books: Affording College in Minnesota*. May 1998. [www.mnplan.state.mn.us/cgi-bin/byteserver.pl/pdf/balance3.pdf].

Robinson, M., and Daigle, S. "Important Lessons from CSU's Failed Strategic Partnership." *Planning for Higher Education*, Winter 1999–2000, 18–31.

Rosevear, S. G. "Lessons for Developing a Partnership-Based Virtual University." *Technology Source*, Apr. 1999. [horizon.unc.edu/TS/vu/1999–04.asp].

Perspective: Glen M. Farrell

A learning marketspace partnership that is successful is based on appreciation of the need for a win-win outcome for all. Membership comes from institutions and organizations that can add value such that the partnership is greater than the sum of its parts. This enables it to respond to market requirements more effectively than can any one member acting alone.

The concept for an LMS partnership is evolving as information becomes more accessible and labor-force requirements grow more dynamic. The evolution is away from exclusively providing course and program products and toward supporting educational planning and learning processes. Partnership services must assist the learner with such functions as setting learning goals; assessing current skills and knowledge; developing appropriate learning plans; identifying quality-assured content providers; maintaining personal learning records; and awarding appropriate credentials such as degrees, diplomas, and certificates.

Decentralization and respect for social and cultural differences also characterize the successful marketspace partnership. Membership includes organizations from the target market regions, with a physical presence in the communities they serve where people can go to access learning technology appliances and engage in face-to-face interaction and group activity.

Influence on Education

Regardless of its genesis, the impact of a marketspace partnership on teaching and learning processes is to add momentum to changes already under way. Indeed, the LMS partnership is only possible because of some of these changes. For example, the once-exclusive franchise of the university to control awarding of higher education credentials, entrance requirements, and the content of the learning agenda has been and continues to be eroded. This unbundling process enables an institution to form a partnership based on functional contributions and, in the process, to demonstrate a new form of virtual institution.

Driving Forces and Obstacles

The goals and aspirations of an institution are the primary driving force regarding membership in an LMS partnership. Membership is a means, not an end. Being able to explain to stakeholders the necessity of joining (and therefore the call to change) in terms of institutional ends makes it easier to deal with the obstacles. But it doesn't make them go away.

Although institutional strategic plans can and should constitute a powerful driving force, the reality is that there are other, often more compelling, forces at work as well. Misperception about the benefits to be gained from partnership is one of them. For example, it is commonly thought that partnering automatically reduces costs. Another fallacy is that technology can simply overlay traditional pedagogy and learner support systems. A decision based on reasons such as these usually ends in disenchantment and rapidly declining commitment to the partnership; however, such reasons can have a powerful influence on administrators who are strapped for resources.

The phenomenon of keeping up with the Joneses is another force currently at work. The ubiquity of the term *virtual education* makes such stakeholders as governors, alumni, and potential students fearful of being left behind. As a result of all these forces, the marketspace partnership may seem attractive for the wrong reasons.

Core processes in educational institutions have evolved with glacial speed over many years and are not susceptible to rapid change. This gives rise to a number of barriers to forming a partnership. Three are particularly noteworthy. First is the nature of curriculum. Historically, it is based on the content knowledge of the expert, not on the needs of the market (as is required in the context of an LMS partnership). Second is the principle of autonomy, which, over the years, has come to be linked with independence. A partnership perceived to threaten independence of decision making may also be seen to undermine autonomy and reduce standards of quality. A third obstacle is that institutions are unable to substantively reallocate existing resources. As a result, innovation tends to happen at the margin and only becomes mainstream once it is judged continuously useful and generating incremental funding to sustain itself.

Leadership

The leaders of an LMS partnership are people of uncommon vision. They are not satisfied with creating course databases in cooperation with other institutions and calling that a virtual college or university. They understand the need to integrate technology with the teaching-and-learning process in ways that go beyond simply delivering courses on the Web or videoconferencing. They understand the importance of being as committed to the success of the common venture as they are to that of their own organization.

These leaders also understand the value of diversity within an educational system and seek ways for the partnership to support it. They understand that the partnering institutions must have a clear vision as to purpose and mandate, measurable indicators of success, and a strategy to move toward the vision. They deal with the question of institutional involvement in LMS partnership in the context of these strategies. In other words, they recognize that involvement in a partnership is not an ad hoc decision.

GLEN M. FARRELL was the founding president and CEO of the Open Learning Agency in British Columbia, Canada. He currently provides consultation and project management services in the areas of technology and change in education systems and organizations.

The Learning Marketspace Toolbox

The central priority in the learning marketspace is to facilitate the cultural shift in learning that characterizes the digital age with its multidimensional networked spaces. In such spaces, there is no limit to how (or how many) people, agents, objects, technologies, and information can relate to one another. Like digital space itself, in which learning is increasingly occurring, the cultural shift in learning is multidimensional. It involves new lifelong learners who learn at different times and in different locations than they used to, continuously congregating in digital spaces to form new learning relationships with other learner-experts.

Much attention has been devoted to the new dimensions of time and space in which digital-age learning occurs, but little attention has been devoted to how the digital age redefines learning itself. Yet, to master the personal and professional challenges of the digital age, learners need to learn new things, and in new ways. In this chapter we examine the cultural shift in digital-age learning and suggest what an LMS portal might look like—what tools it might provide—to facilitate this cultural shift in learning.

The Cultural Shift in Learning

With their unlimited dimensions, potential for amassing information, and capacity for building relationships and connections, digital spaces raise a number of technical and ethical issues for knowledge development, management, and sharing—in short, for learning (see Figure 5.1 for an overview). Specifically, it is now possible to develop unprecedented amounts of digital information about individuals—information that can be created, searched, transferred, processed, manipulated, matched, and combined with other information in mere seconds. In the predigital age, this generation, manipulation, and use of information was simply unthinkable. Consequently, organizations could easily manage the small amount of static information (usually paper-based) that was available. Institutional management of individuals' information did not cause space or management problems, nor did information management result in seemingly insurmountable ethical problems.

But as a consequence of institution-based management of personal information and knowledge in the industrial age, people overall are passive in managing their own information and knowledge. In fact, it is common practice for individuals to expect all kinds of institutions to manage their personal information. For example, legal institutions manage birth certificates and other personal documents; health care institutions manage our health records, X rays, and genetic information; and educational institutions manage our educational records, certifications, memberships in student organizations, and so on.

Most people seldom think about owning or managing their personal information, or making decisions as to who is allowed access to it or how to share their knowledge and information. Currently, if people need access to their own information, they must request it from the institutions that manage it.

In the digital age, however, the amount and versatility of information about individuals explodes, potentially including such sensitive information as one's DNA. In fact, computer scientists speak of the emergence of a "digital persona" (Clarke, 1994; Agre, 1998). We are only beginning to experience the possibilities of information manipulation. As Agre points out, "the techniques for . . . using

Figure 5.1. The Cultural Shift to Personal Information and Knowledge Management in the Digital Age

	Industrial (Paper) Age	Digital Age (Industrial-age knowledge management)	Digital Age (Digital-age knowledge management)
Management	• Institutions manage personal information of individuals in paper-based record systems, such as file cabinets.	• Institutions manage personal information of individuals in electronic databases.	• Individuals manage their personal information in a personal electronic system.
Access	• Institutions control access to information; individuals must request their own information from the managing institution.	• Institutions control access to information more efficiently; individuals must request their own information from the managing institution.	• Individuals control access to and manage their personal information any time and from any place.
Manipulation	• The potential for searching, matching, exchanging, or selling an individual's personal information is limited.	• The potential for searching, matching, exchanging, and selling an individual's personal information is unlimited.	• The potential for searching, matching, exchanging, and selling an individual's personal information is controlled by the individual.
Implications for higher education	• Institutions control learning processes and records.	• Institutions control learning processes and records electronically, but also encounter the quantitative and ethical limits of industrial-age knowledge management in the digital age.	• Learners control learning processes, products, and records in a dynamic personal knowledge management system (new pedagogy and technologies).

Source: Based on a series of conversations with Paul Treuer, University of Minnesota, Duluth, Mar. 2000.

. . . databases [of personal information] . . . have multiplied. Data-mining algorithms, for example, can extract commercially mean-ingful patterns from extremely large amounts of information" (1998, p. 3).

To give just one example of the problems involved in mixing and matching digital information, consider the case of a Maryland banker who accessed medical records to find clients diagnosed with cancer so as to recall their loans (see American Civil Liberties Union Privacy Web site, www.aclu.org/privacy, Dec. 2000). Clearly, an industrial-age, institution-based style of managing personal infor-mation is obsolete. Individuals need to learn how to take active control of and responsibility for owning and managing their own information and knowledge. With regard to health care, individu-als need to own and manage all their health records, including diag-nostic reports, X rays, drug prescriptions, medical history, possible programming of medical devices, DNA information, and so on. Individuals need to learn how to share such information responsi-bly, as in creating a version of this information customized for use by a doctor anywhere in the world they deem appropriate.

At the same time, the sheer amount of digital information about an individual makes it increasingly difficult for institutions to man-age it. Professionals in higher education have been alerting us to the crisis in information technology support since the mid-1990s (Yohe, 1996; McClure and others, 1997). In the learning market-space, with learning opportunities accumulated from multiple part-ners, the problem of information management intensifies. How do institutions keep up with these learners? How do learners manage, integrate, and present the competencies gained from these diverse learning experiences? Clearly, the shift from institutional to indi-vidual management of knowledge and information is inevitable.

Despite this cultural shift in knowledge management and learn-ing to individual control, most institutions of higher education continue to pour large amounts of resources into improving indus-trial-age forms of institution-based knowledge management and control, to keep up with the explosion in information and knowledge. As D. Quinn Mills and Janet Pumo (1999) write, "Unfortunately, what we are not seeing is a direct relationship between the administrative efficiencies and an increased investment in the academic applications of IT. When institutions are embarking upon wholesale replacements of their core administrative applications, to the tune of tens of millions of dollars each, and when they are streamlining their administrative business processes, these initiatives rarely promise to directly reallocate a portion of these savings to academic applications of technology" (pp. 292–293). Although most of these systems take advantage of digital technology to improve the efficiency of the institution's management processes, they merely reproduce industrial-age, institution-based approaches.

However, as control over information and knowledge management is renegotiated among institutions and individuals, technologies favoring institutional control increasingly lose the capacity to meet learners' needs as well as those of the institution. They grow less viable as learners discover the unlimited possibility for learning relationships in digital space and move more and more easily from one learning provider to another and select exactly the learning opportunities they need.

An LMS portal must therefore provide a tool that allows learners to take control of managing and sharing their knowledge, information, and learning processes. Such a dynamic electronic system for managing personal knowledge has to be built on a philosophy of learner control and managed lifelong learning.

New Tools Needed

Higher education needs to lead the way and develop new pedagogy and curricula for these new individual competencies. On the one hand, learners need to learn new things. Given the ethical and technical exigencies in the digital age, they must learn how to own, manage, and share their lifelong learning and professional information. For example, they should learn how to reflect on their knowledge and effectively demonstrate their competencies for any educational institution to consider (as in degree-auditing processes) or for employers to evaluate for hiring or professional development opportunities.

On the other hand, to acquire these new approaches, individuals must learn in a new way, by controlling their own learning process. As institutions move to the learning marketspace and develop the pedagogy and curricula needed for the cultural shift in digital-age learning, we see three sets of tools facilitating this shift:

1. *Information and access tools*. These permit access to aggregated information about higher education and employment.

2. *Streamlined and shared services tools*. These manage common credit transfer, registration, admissions, and other standards and procedures.

3. *Relationship tools*. These are for acquiring knowledge through learning relationships. This group comprises e-portfolios, e-mentoring, and e-learning communities.

We believe relationships to be the number one priority of the learning marketspace. This third set of tools, then, helps to overcome the sometimes intimidating impersonal and mass-oriented feeling encountered in megaportals. Because of the heavy investment in personal learning relationships in addition to communications technologies, the third set of tools can be achieved only through partnership.

Information and Access

An LMS partnership should afford seamless access to the career, course, job, and business resources needed by all learners. One such project, a partnership of nine Minnesota state educational organizations and institutions called the Internet System for Education and Employment Knowledge (ISEEK, www.iseek.org), is a model for using technology to enhance and align a learner's career assessment, course choices, and future business opportunities.

This basic tool gives learners, counselors, and employers a virtual advising office for help with needs assessment, program identification, and financial aid, as well as a common catalogue for links to courses and class schedule information (potentially from all providers in the partnership). In addition, employers, community groups, and learners of any age or at any location can post requests regarding their specific learning needs and preferred delivery method (face-to-face, Web, interactive television, and so forth), and a match is then made between provider and learner.

Streamlined and Shared Services

An institution should also partner to better standardize its credit transfer policies and develop technologies that allow learners to move easily from one learning provider to another. One initiative, known as the Course Applicability System (CAS, www.transfer.org) allows students to input their course records and immediately learn where their courses transfer, across partnering institutions and states.

Participating institutions in Ohio, Arizona, California, Washington, Wisconsin, and Oregon are beginning to partner on such an initiative to enhance transferability across systems. The institutions in this partnership are building a prototype Web application that "will assist students, advisors, faculty, and administrators from two-year colleges and universities to obtain consistent and accurate information about transfer courses and [their] applicability toward degree completion" (daraix01.mcs.muohio.edu/cas, Dec. 2000). In addition, CAS uses the Web to enhance communications between faculty and staff who are responsible for making transfer articulation decisions. The goal is an efficient, accessible, and online process to help transfer students move from school to school and earn a degree in a timely manner.

To build an account, the learner chooses the state and institution where he or she would like the account to reside. A learner transferring to another institution can continue using the same account.

Learners expect an institution of higher learning to accept courses from any accredited institution. A school with a clearly stated credit transfer policy and tools such as CAS in place does indeed have a marketable edge. As Murray Turoff (2000) observes, "There are no longer geographical monopolies on higher education. Only consortiums based upon real cooperation among the participating institutions will succeed. Many current attempts to market only the separate offerings of the participating institutions, or to impose layers of administration between the courses and the students, are doomed to a marketplace failure."

Relationships

We know that a higher education partnership must leverage the best content created by the partners and establish a seamless gateway so that learners can access the content from any number of entry points. But along with the need to streamline services comes the pressing human need of encouraging and supporting learning relationships. As research on pedagogy consistently points out, learning relationships are crucial for creating knowledge. In the digital age, with learners having to learn how to take control of their learning process, these relationships are simply indispensable. We propose three basic relationship-building tools: personal digital knowledge management systems (e-portfolios), e-mentors, and e-learning communities.

Personal Digital Management Systems (E-Portfolios)

The personal digital management system—a technology that will help learners develop, manage, integrate, and share their information and knowledge with others—will be a critical tool of a learning marketspace. We envision this technology to be an online, cross-functional, learner-controlled personal learning and career development system designed to help learners become responsible and active managers of their knowledge and competencies by putting the control of their learning and career development in their hands. For lack of a better term, we call it *e-portfolio*, but another descriptor (though an unwieldy one) captures it well as a dynamic, integrated, electronic learning management system.

Rather than merely settling for presenting learner information and data as stored at an institution, the e-portfolio concept focuses on how the learner can best use this information to become a successful lifelong learner. It allows learners to integrate knowledge, competencies, resources, services, credentials, projects, assessment results—anything they need to plan, track, and present their learning and work.

An e-portfolio enables the learner to create, access, store, and selectively display educational, professional, and personal records, including demonstration of competencies (by way of drawings, photographs, writing samples, performance videos, test results, and credentials). Learners can create customized versions of their records and send them in seconds to a selected audience, such as course team members, a counselor, an admissions officer, faculty, an employer, and others. Specifically, the e-portfolio

- Enables learners to take full control and responsibility for their learning and career development processes and data

- Motivates learners to become (and stay) involved in lifelong learning and work processes

- Improves learning outcomes by enabling competency-based, outcome-oriented contractual learning

- Enables learners to build, assess, track, reflect on, articulate, and demonstrate their competencies, thus increasing their potential to develop careers and find employment

Electronic Learning Portfolio at the University of Minnesota

Why should the university, rather than the individual, maintain records about a student's cocurricular activities? In the digital age, the individual can and should be calculated in the formula for distributing and managing his or her personal information. The issues are entitlement and control. Each individual is entitled to easy, full, and direct access to personal records and influence over their distribution and use. But how do we make the shift from institutional control of personal information to owner control?

The answer is twofold: first, create tools that make it possible for individuals to distribute and manage personal information, and second, teach them the necessary skills to use these tools responsibly.

An initiative at the University of Minnesota (U of M) is beginning to address this need. Portfolio 2.0 (see the screenshot) is the second phase in developing an electronic learning portfolio: an Internet repository with sufficient storage to host an individual's official records, self-reported information, and multimedia files containing work samples. Portfolio 2.0 constitutes a secure computing environment with links to system databases. Its security system is the same as that for other educational records; entries are encrypted and password-protected using U of M usernames and passwords. Users can manage their educational records by creating customized views of their own Portfolio account to share with other individuals for specific purposes, such as academic advisement or employment. The process of sharing records is also password-protected.

Portfolio 2.0 is a tool providing for both formative and summative processes. As a tool for formative processes, each user can use the Portfolio 2.0 account to build an ever-growing compilation of learning documents and records. This formative process of accumulating materials representing intellectual growth is intended to be lifelong.

In addition, Portfolio 2.0 can be used at any time for summative purposes as a snapshot, useful for a specific individual or group. For example, a student may create an advising view of the portfolio consisting of snail-mail, e-mail, and Web addresses; photograph; official academic records; an essay describing academic goals; degree program requirements; academic plan; résumé; and multimedia work samples.

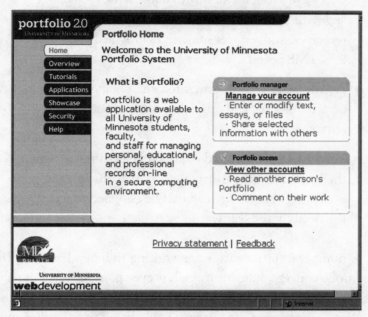

The prospect of using an electronic learning portfolio extends beyond the university. A partnership between an educational institution and the workplace is enhanced when a portfolio view is transferred electronically from one learning environment to another. To this end, it benefits multiple learning communities to use electronic portfolios having similar standards for layout, organization, and data fields. Common portfolio standards give users a powerful tool for managing accurate, useful records, before, during, and after the college experience. In this way learners can document and manage lifelong educational records continuously, regardless of institutional affiliation.

If the role of education is to empower graduates to be informed, responsible citizens, perhaps the most important lesson to be taught—given the current state of the digital information revolution—is that one can manage one's own personal information effectively and efficiently. Otherwise it will be difficult, perhaps impossible, in the digital age to demonstrate the most important trait of a learned person: knowledge of oneself.

PAUL TREUER
Associate Professor, Supportive Services Program
University of Minnesota, Duluth

- Gives learners a useful way to make sense of and apply the potentially confusing range of information, resources, and services sometimes provided at a large LMS portal

- Permits access to all learner records, competency demonstrations, and other data, anytime and anywhere

- Encourages personalized contractual learning, in which the learner and the instructor negotiate and plan how a learning opportunity can best be designed to meet the needs of the learner

A number of universities are working independently on the e-portfolio concept. In many cases, however, portfolio services replicate the structural segregation of traditional support and service functions, transferring them from a paper-based to an online environment. In essence, the majority of higher education institutions currently represent themselves and their information with less-than-stellar concern, support, or guidance for lifelong learners, let alone for what and how they need to learn to make the cultural shift in digital learning. The medium may be new, but the modes of interaction and locus of control remain the same. In contrast, note Paul Treuer's accompanying description of an innovative e-portfolio. You can access an example portfolio at portfolio.umn.edu.

The E-Mentor Concept

As learners control and manage more of their own information and knowledge, educational institutions must help learners do so actively and responsibly. Although the e-portfolio can be the technological centerpiece in this process, that technology alone is not enough. In the process of helping learners become responsible knowledge and learning managers, the e-mentor is an indispensable agent in developing and implementing the pedagogy that facilitates this cultural shift for the learner. The e-mentor fulfills the crucial relationship link between the learner and the institution.

The e-mentor concept focuses on connecting the learner with a K–12 or higher education institution strategically by way of an e-mentor at the institution. The primary goal of the e-mentor is to increase the quality and quantity of learner-controlled and learner-managed e-learning and achievement. Potentially, every learner can be connected with an e-mentor for the purpose of meeting lifelong learning needs.

An e-mentor is an individual or group at an institution (or more than one) that guides a learner in achieving his or her goals. In this discussion, a learner may be an individual or even a business, industry, or group. The e-mentor is available online at the LMS portal. He or she works with the advisors, counselors, and faculty available at the local institution, workforce development center, extension office, local library, bookstore, and so on.

Instead of requiring that the learner come to a specific institution, the e-mentor focuses on establishing a relationship with the learner, understanding the learning need, and finding the best match between learning resources and the learner. Specifically, an association or business indicates the competencies needed, and the learner brings his or her current education, training, and experience in the form of an e-portfolio.

The e-mentor then helps to identify the gap between what the learner knows and needs to know; the mentor also identifies the educational resources available and those needed from a variety of entities (higher education institution, corporation, and so on) to meet the learning need. The e-mentor helps the learner identify the best delivery mode (face-to-face, online synchronous, online asynchronous), critical content, and e-learning resources that meet the learning need. In short, the e-mentor helps the learner

- Locate e-learning resources that directly meet his or her needs

- Identify learning gaps and locate resources and e-faculty who can help

- Develop a personal learning plan (e-portfolio)

- Set up an ongoing assessment and achievement plan (progress monitoring)

- Become a responsible and active manager of his or her own information and knowledge

The E-Learning Community

The e-learning community provides yet another important set of relationships and connections for learners in a learning market-space. Considering the unprecedented pace of change in knowledge, technology, and society, learners need to expand their ways of learning to include learning from peers and colleagues. Increasingly, learners are understood as experts, while experts are recognized as being learners themselves, resulting in their learning from each other. Consequently, they need to have the opportunity to interact with other learner-experts in the learning marketspace. Only through interaction with these other learners can new benchmarks for digital-age learning develop, such as those for knowledge management and e-portfolio development.

Mary Bauman (1997) notes that the e-learning community is a place where learners can test assumptions, try out new ideas, and ask difficult questions by way of the company and support of other learners: "Online learning communities mirror the kinds of learning communities we find on college campuses where an effort is made to enrich students' experience beyond the classroom walls, via support services such as the library, writing centers and other tutoring help; via cultural enrichment such as programs which invite outside speakers to campus, film programs, concerts and the like; and via the common spaces which exist on any physical campus—the student union, the cafeteria, a commons at the center of campus, or the library, to name a few possibilities."

Despite the significance of the learning relationship built in such a community, few LMSs currently offer such opportunities. Our survey of sites revealed that only a few invest in relationships through learning communities. If they do (as in the case of Hungry Minds), they tend to limit their offers to a Web chat board or similar technology. Investing in human relationships and using these technologies to organize and develop a learning community remain a scarce undertaking, despite the integral role of learning relationships in creating knowledge.

Conclusion

John Seely Brown, chief scientist at Xerox and director of its Palo Alto Research Center, writes: "The real literacy of tomorrow entails the ability to be your own personal reference librarian—to know how to navigate through confusing, complex information spaces and feel comfortable doing so. 'Navigation' may well be the main form of literacy for the twenty-first century" (2000, p. 14).

To enable learners to navigate, own, and manage their learning, a learning marketspace—with its aggregated learning opportunities—requires a cultural shift from institution-controlled, mass learning processes to learner-controlled, individualized learning experiences. This shift obligates moving away from the currently predominant Web model that reproduces existing institutional structures and processes, to a relationship model that connects the learner with other learners, institutions, and e-mentors and shifts the locus of control over knowledge management to the learner.

The toolbox that we suggest in this chapter supports this shift in three important ways. The e-portfolio is a dynamic electronic learning management system that enables learners to take control of their learning process and to share their educational process and products with others. The e-mentor fulfills the crucial relationship link between the learner and the educational and career resources and services. Finally, the e-learning community is an expanded set of learning relationships in support of developing new benchmarks for learning.

The necessary technologies and learning relationships for digital-age learning require a heavy investment, one that an individual institution may not be able to afford by itself. Again, institutions can partner to revolutionize career planning, learning, teaching, and advising processes and to build the basis for wide-ranging institutional change. Through an LMS partnership, an institution can leverage its resources to negotiate the opportunities and constraints involved in building a successful learning infrastructure that facilitates the cultural shift to digital-age learning and knowledge management.

References

Agre, P. "Introduction." In P. Agre and M. Rotenberg (eds.), *Technology and Privacy: The New Landscape*. Cambridge, Mass.: MIT Press, 1998.

American Civil Liberties Union. "Privacy." Apr. 1999. [www.aclu.org/privacy, Dec. 2000].

Bauman, M. "Online Learning Communities." *Trends and Issues in Online Instruction*, second annual Teaching in the Community Colleges Online conference, Apr. 1–3, 1997. [leahi.kcc.hawaii.edu/org/tcc_conf97/pres/bauman.html].

Brown, J. S. "Growing Up Digital: How the Web Changes Work, Education, and the Ways People Learn." *Change*, Mar.–Apr. 2000, pp. 11–20.

Clarke, R. "The Digital Persona and Its Application to Data Surveillance." *Information Society*, 1994, *10*(2), 77–92.

McClure, P., and others. *The Crisis in Information Technology Support: Has Our Current Model Reached Its Limit?* Boulder, Colo.: CAUSE, 1997. [www.educause.edu/ir/library/pdf/pub3016.pdf].

Mills, D. Q., and Pumo, J. M. "Managing Change in Higher Education: A Leader's Guide." In R. N. Katz and D. G. Oblinger (eds.), *Renewing Administration: Preparing Colleges and Universities for the 21st Century*. Bolton, Mass.: Anker, 1999.

Turoff, M. "An End to Student Segregation: No More Separation Between Distance Learning and Regular Courses." *On the Horizon*, 2000, 8(1), 1–7.

Yohe, M. "Information Technology Support Services: Crisis or Opportunity?" *CAUSE/EFFECT*, Fall 1996, pp. 6–13.

Perspective: Murray Turoff

Successful learning marketspace partnerships are ones in which all the participants contribute what they are best suited to contribute. These are programs in a given field in which the college and university environment has a solid foundation of both undergraduate accreditation and graduate programs with a healthy research component on the part of faculty. They include industry participation to expose students (through co-op and intern programs) and faculty to current industrial practice and problems. They encourage industry involvement in college and university research efforts.

It is probably easier to state what such programs should *not* look like:

- They are not programs where industry attempts to set educational standards or replace the educational experience that should be obtained from a college curriculum.

- They are not university programs based upon a profit motive, and they are not attempts by a university to provide just-in-time learning and other skills training.

- They do not offer expensive executive degrees with little or no homework or responsibility for learning on the part of the student.

- They are not programs where the college or university subordinates the needs and objectives of the students to those of industry.

- They are not programs where the distance student is treated differently from the regular student, or educated by adjuncts other than the regular faculty of the institution.

- They are not programs in which the regular faculty has no responsibility to determine the long-term educational objectives on a basis insensitive to the latest fads in the marketplace.

Influence on Education

The geographic monopoly that many institutions have on educational delivery (whether public, private, or for-profit training) is dead, or at least dying. It is now possible to get any sort of college or university degree, or any sort of training curriculum, from anywhere in the world where there is an institution offering it. Furthermore, the cost of education is comparable to what an individual would spend to buy a car every year. For cars, there are all sorts of detailed evaluation reports the consumer can pay for to obtain the information needed to make an informed decision. So, too, the greatest impact of the new technologies of distance education will be the emergence of student consumerism and resulting demand for value in the educational offerings chosen.

Driving Forces and Obstacles

The driving force is the growing recognition that the information economy and the enterprise nature of business and consumer relationships require not only an initial education but one that is continuous and lifelong. The obstacle is the warped view that learning comes from recorded lectures given by Nobel prize winners, and that having just anyone—or a computer—grade assignments is sufficient to provoke or assess learning accomplishment.

Delivering a quality education is still a product of small classes (whether virtual or face-to-face) and hard work on the part of a talented teacher who can promote a student's active learning as well as collaborative learning among the students as a group and a class. It is not the "venture investors'" dream of single classes of a thousand students, watching a video of a leading expert while an army of cheap teaching assistants grade individual assignments via e-mail. The profit motive is the leading obstacle to any rational investment in the future of education.

Another major obstacle—just as blind to the future—is the Luddite-oriented educator who has mastered the "sage on the stage" form of classroom education and feels there is no way to reach and motivate students other than the face-to-face environment.

The final obstacle is the formal educator who wishes to maintain distance and formality between himself and the students. This form of educational delivery will never succeed in the communication-rich environment of the Web. Educators who prefer to maintain an aloof atmosphere with their students and who refuse to change their attitude toward using technology should not be pushed into attempting to offer any form of distance education.

Timing

An organization should embark on a partnership effort when the resulting enterprise serves the educational goals of the institution, which must first and primarily be to serve the interests of the students. Once the other partners recognize the primary nature of that mission to be the very foundation of what a college or university is, then the partnership can proceed.

MURRAY TUROFF is Distinguished Professor of Computer and Information Science at the New Jersey Institute of Technology.

6

The Partnering Process
A Case Study of Minnesota Virtual University

The exigencies for partnering to build a learning marketspace are compelling. On the one hand, the winner-take-all environment of the marketspace makes partnering a question of survival for the institutions involved. Without strategic partnership, an individual institution will find it difficult to compete with the mega-marketspaces that are emerging on the higher education landscape. On the other hand, the urgency of partnering extends far beyond the needs of individual institutions; indeed, it is about learners, about intellectual and social capital. In short, the necessity arises from the social contract that the educational institution maintains with digital-age society.

Despite these strong calls for partnering, the process involved in building a strategic partnership for an LMS can be complex and difficult. To some extent, this complexity results from the missions, values, and priorities of greatly differing organizations as well as from their individual stages of readiness (see Chapters Three and Four). In this chapter, we analyze these complexities and describe the practical work of building such a partnership by way of a longitudinal case study of how the Minnesota Virtual University was constructed. Specifically, we show how priorities, readiness criteria, and the nature of a learning marketspace as a disruptive innovation bear on the partnership process. The discussion that follows owes much to the seminal work of Clayton Christensen (1997), the Harvard

Business School scholar who developed the theory of sustaining and disruptive technology-based innovations (see discussion in Chapter Two).

The Learning Marketspace as a Disruptive Innovation

According to Christensen, an innovation is disruptive because it outpaces customer demand for performance improvement in the mainstream market. The learning marketspace, then, is a disruptive innovation because it appeals to customers who have traditionally not been considered mainstream (such as adult and lifelong learners), and once fully developed, it becomes more appealing to current mainstream learners as well. In addition, today's fringe learners become tomorrow's mainstream learners.

Disruptive innovation brings about revolutionary change in organizations and people's lives in revolutionary ways, but it is often vague, misunderstood, or even ignored or rejected—especially by large organizations. This revolutionary change is based on a radically new value proposition. In the learning marketspace, the new value proposition is an increase in learner control over the learning process. To address the learning needs of individuals, communities, and organizations, these values require new processes, such as rapid response. Furthermore, an LMS partnership requires serious investment in technology and learning relationships, which often turns the marketspace into an unpopular competitor for existing resources.

Although the concepts of disruptive and sustaining technologies were originally devised in the province of business and management theory, they are useful in understanding the dynamics of LMS partnership processes as well. Christensen describes an "innovator's dilemma," whereby the strong advantages gained by moving fast to embrace disruptive innovation are offset by great risk because of how little is known about the market. This dilemma has been clearly visible in the process of building the Minnesota Virtual University.

Evolution of the Minnesota Virtual University

The Minnesota Virtual University, or MnVU (see Figure 6.1), is a statewide learning marketspace first announced in 1996 by then-Governor Arne Carlson. A year later, in the midst of a heated national (and international) debate about the future of higher education, the Minnesota legislature passed a Higher Education Bill that called for the establishment of a statewide virtual university. Section 34 describes this initiative as "a public-private partnership consisting of the University of Minnesota, MnSCU [Minnesota State Colleges and Universities] and private colleges and universities [developing] . . . an electronic system that will support access to instructional, support, and administrative services" ("Omnibus . . . ," 1997).

Figure 6.1. Minnesota Virtual University

A chronology serves as a brief overview of the response to this bill:

- *Fall 1997.* The MnVU Coordinating Board and several committees are founded.

- *Spring 1998.* A project manager is hired, and the Student Services Committee initiates the MnVU Web site with the help of a design firm.

- *Summer 1998.* MnVU prototypes are designed and tested.

- *Fall 1998.* Twelve task teams are formed to address various aspects of the initiative (for example, service facilitation, partnerships, and K–12 connections).

- *Spring 1999.* Operations manager and support staff are hired. The Web site moves from the design firm's server to one at a participating organization.

- *Summer 1999.* MnVU is released as a test site.

- *Fall 1999.* MnVU partners with ISEEK (Minnesota's Internet System for Education and Employment).

- *Spring 2000.* MnVU begins a revision-and-redesign phase.

For the state, the stakes in this project are high. Minnesota is home to a large number of high-tech industries. Nevertheless, attracting and fostering new start-up business in these industries has become increasingly difficult. Recent economic figures indicate that "Minnesota's share of national initial public stock offerings shrunk from 6.8 percent to 1.5 percent in . . . [1999], and the state's share of venture capital, the primary source of startup money for new companies, dropped from 3 percent in 1995 to 1.3 percent in . . . [1999]" (Smetanka, 2000).

If Minnesota intends to maintain its current economic prosperity and support high-tech industries, there must be a highly visible and accessible learning marketspace with an excellent reputation for digital-age learning. To be sure, such an infrastructure alone does not ensure economic prosperity, but it is an important strategic piece of economic development in the digital economy. As Janet Caldow points out, "tax investment incentives, e-business taxation policy, digital contract law, e-business education and training—it's all part of a carefully planned, economic development strategy" (1999).

In the fall of 1997, four design committees were formed: a coordinating board, a student services and design team, a quality-in-learning team, and a technology team. These administrators, faculty, librarians, student services professionals, students, and private sector representatives began constructing the Minnesota Virtual University. A year later, twelve task teams including more than one hundred people were working on strategic aspects of MnVU, such as a facilitation plan, a rapid-response mechanism for customized training requests, K–12 connections, and more. All the groups were brought together several times a year to present and discuss their work and to develop a sense of shared ownership of the learning marketspace.

This approach was designed to address the disruptive nature of the innovation. Given its new value propositions and its competition for existing resources, MnVU was susceptible to the same risk of failure as any other disruptive innovation. Investment in shared ownership and a broad participatory base were essential to divert attempts by a few powerful entities to stop the initiative or redirect it into structures that would merely reproduce existing institutional structures.

Performance Dynamics

A disruptive innovation usually underperforms existing counterparts in a mainstream market—at least in the initial stages of development—

and as a result is usually unfavorably compared to competing offerings. This is true for MnVU as well. It currently offers a common course catalogue of services at the information-and-access stage (see Chapter Five). But compared to MnVU, existing universities offer much more: registration, admissions, programs, degrees, financial aid, and counseling.

Potentially, MnVU can offer all these services from a large number of diverse institutions in a more scalable and flexible way, to extend access to more learners and even go beyond these services. The virtual university can create new learning opportunities, leverage resources through one-on-one mentoring relationships, and ultimately foster learner control over the learning process. However, at this point, MnVU's performance seems inferior in comparison to that of other institutions. It then becomes important for the partners to understand the disruptive nature of the innovation. Without awareness of the expected initial underperformance, participants may have little patience for the innovation and abandon it.

Return on Investment

It is especially difficult for large organizations such as universities to embrace disruptive innovation, because in their attempt to satisfy their current mainstream market they often have little interest in investing in a market that currently has only a small percentage of the customers they need to sustain themselves. Again, this is true for MnVU. So long as there is a sufficient number of campus-bound learners, the large organizations participating in MnVU are not likely to pursue interest in an innovation designed to serve an emerging market. The demand for more accessible and affordable forms of higher education is thus seen as minimal.

Consequently, resources needed for the success of an innovation of the MnVU sort tend to be redirected to projects that sustain and improve the performance of existing operations. This concern was salient for at least one university executive in the

MnVU experience, who questioned whether the $2.5 million budget allocated for the project would be better spent building core academic programs.

Indeed, that development partner opted to redirect half of a legislative appropriation for MnVU to projects that sustain and improve the performance of that institution's existing operations. This issue of directing resources away from disruptive innovation further highlights the readiness criterion of being sure that leadership is committed to the innovation.

Ambiguity and Emerging Markets

Since disruptive innovation tends to appeal to fringe customers or emerging markets, analyzing these markets is important yet difficult. Market, value, benefits, and consequences of a disruptive innovation are ambiguous and vague. As Christensen found, this difficulty in grasping the ultimate point of a disruptive innovation often paralyzes administrators and leaders, despite their customary success in managing sustaining innovation: "They [executives] demand market data when none exists and make judgments based upon financial projections when neither revenues or costs can, in fact, be known. *Using planning and marketing techniques that were developed to manage sustaining technologies in the very different context of disruptive ones is an exercise in flapping wings*" (1997, pp. xxi–xxii; italics added).

In the process of designing MnVU, this notion of vagueness and ambiguity surfaced many times. At a design meeting two years into the project, members of the design committee continued to discuss the value of the innovation. They were grappling with difficult questions that we might paraphrase this way: "It's not something that has caught fire with our administration. It's the value thing. What's the benefit to the institution? Is there a way to track how many students come through the site? What does success look like? Do we need to market this to the institutions again?" Participants were asking questions whose answers, in fact, could not be known in the same way they would in a traditional sustaining environment.

Given MnVU's great variety of participating organizations and stakeholders, the initial conceptions were just as wide-ranging. A business representative, for example, viewed MnVU as a way to "extend the brand" to "learners of all ages throughout Minnesota and eventually the entire world." A faculty member thought students and businesses would see in it "an electronic way of looking at what possible options they have for . . . continuing education." A representative from a technology company wanted MnVU to deliver "the services of the . . . sixty-eight universities and colleges in Minnesota virtually"; for him the problem was, "How do we come up with a piece of technology that we're going to agree on for a standard?"

Administrators and executives from larger organizations tended to consider MnVU as "the front door to higher education in Minnesota," with the implication that there would be few if any structural changes behind the new entryway. Similarly, one university executive perhaps sensing the prospect of deep change, adhered to the belief that the technology was merely a "way to present a coherent picture" of his institution. And an executive of a private educational institution chose to focus on giving "real access to the most impoverished in our societies and allow them to climb the ladder to economic and social stability."

Divergence was the hallmark of attempts to name the partnership as well. During the course of several naming sessions, the partners discarded some names because they sounded too similar to one institution or another, and others because there simply was insufficient consensus on the partnership's expected outcomes. That is, the partners could not determine the implications of the innovation for their institutions and for the future of higher education in general. They each came to the table with very different expectations of what the partnership would deliver. MnVU is considered the current working name, but it still causes discomfort among partners.

This process has mostly been one of discovery and disclosure, requiring a substantial amount of tolerance for ambiguity. Partners must promote discovery and disclosure because early attempts to pinpoint specific implications of the innovation often result in the initial rejection of any structural change. Consequently, the result remains a focus on traditional structures and values that serve mainstream customers. Tolerance for ambiguity is necessary to make the shift from traditional ways of learning to building a learning marketspace. Only amid such ambiguity can an LMS partnership move beyond information and access.

Revisiting Priorities and Readiness

Disruptive innovation affects essentially every division of an organization and accentuates many of the difficulties of getting organizations to work together. MnVU is a statewide partnership among public and private colleges and universities, private proprietary institutions, the private sector, libraries, government offices, and so on—all with their own values, goals, motivations, concerns, traditions, strategies, needs, and readiness criteria.

This challenge inevitably surfaced as the partners, undertaking the design process, wrestled with the conception each participating organization had of its own role and that of the collaborators. The spectrum ranged from fear and concern to openness and need for a participatory approach. Several design team members saw that need in terms of getting buy-in from the institutions and faculty. Yet one administrator envisioned his public university very much in a leadership position, ready to determine the roles of the other partners and wary of his institution having to give up too much. This was a far cry from another university executive's belief that MnVU would be "the best collaboration yet in higher education in Minnesota."

These examples illustrate the complexity and ambiguity involved in developing an LMS partnership such as the Minnesota Virtual University.

Summary

In many cases, a learning marketspace assumes the characteristics of a disruptive innovation. Directed at the emerging market of life-long learners, the LMS partnership must redefine current institutional structures in higher education rather than merely reproduce brick-and-mortar structures in an online medium. Disruptive change is unavoidable in building a learning infrastructure that can meet the needs of the new lifelong learner.

At the same time, the disruptive nature of an LMS partnership requires new processes, values, and resources, which render its design a complex challenge. However the partnering organizations decide to address this challenge, successful innovation of this sort depends on the unequivocal commitment of the leadership. Where leadership commitment was lacking, none of the many disruptive innovations Christensen studied was successful. None.

As a legislative mandate, though, MnVU had no choice but to go forward notwithstanding lack of commitment. The questions therefore remain: What alternatives do institutions that cannot reject their social contract of serving citizens and organizations have, if leadership is not committed to the innovation? Can a broad participatory process serve as a sufficient catalyst to make an LMS partnership a success?

References

Caldow, J. "E-Communities, Portals, and the Public Sector." Center for E-Communities, Institute for Electronic Government, IBM, 1999. [www.ieg.ibm.com/pubs/ecomm.html].

Christensen, C. *The Innovator's Dilemma: When New Technologies Cause Great Firms to Fail.* Boston: Harvard Business School Press, 1997.

"Omnibus Higher Education Funding Bill." S.F. 1888. Minnesota State Legislature, May 15, 1997. [www.senate.leg.state.mn.us/departments/scr/billsumm/1997–98/SF1888.htm].

Smetanka, M. "Yudof Plans High-Tech Summit." startribune.com, Apr. 6, 2000. [www.startribune.com].

Perspective: Diana G. Oblinger

The learning marketspace partnership concept rests on the notion that performance (research, e-learning, and so forth) can be significantly improved through joint action. A true partnership relationship has among its characteristics risk sharing and the need to view the relationship as a series of exchanges with no definite endpoint, as well as the need to establish mechanisms to monitor the venture.

Good partnerships include the following:

- Trust that all parties share the same goals. Trust and confidence are built up through a working relationship or through specific partnership activities.

- Partners taking care of each other. The relationship moves from a rhetoric of partnership to a relationship of mutual dependence.

- Partners sharing common assumptions about the business. Everyone understands where it is going, what kind of environment they are operating in, and how best to approach problems together.

- Partners each understanding how the others work. It takes time to educate one another; the key is sharing knowledge.

- Effective partners bringing distinctive resources to the relationship. They are building something greater than any partner can do alone.

- Each party bringing skills and specific knowledge to the enterprise.

Influence on Education

In a world that is so increasingly complex, no single individual or organization is likely to have all the expertise (or resources) it needs to be successful. Increasingly, higher education must work with partners, both inside and outside the academy.

Ultimately, partnership makes higher education stronger as well as more responsive. In the world of e-business, speed, innovation, and flexibility are key characteristics. If we learn to work with new players, we can bring new talents and perspectives to our most pressing challenges. This helps us respond quickly and with great innovation and flexibility.

Obstacles

Our biggest obstacles in building partnerships may be traced back to unchallenged assumptions about higher education. Most of us, as individuals and institutions, feel that we must do it all. This assumption must be challenged if we are to have a successful partnership. There is sometimes another assumption, that not-for-profit is superior to for-profit. This too may limit our ability to partner. Challenging our assumptions surely helps us partner more effectively.

Our institutions tend to avoid risk—for very good reasons. Although there is risk in developing a new relationship, one of the major advantages of a partnership is risk aversion, or risk sharing. We must accept a certain amount of risk to capture any benefit.

Communication of expectations is critical. Many relationships fail because the parties do not communicate clearly; expectations are vague or are not articulated clearly to everyone involved. In the absence of information, people create their own set of expectations. If expectations are not clearly communicated, it is likely that neither party's expectations will be met. Thus each side feels disappointed in the relationship.

Timing

All parties in the potential partnership should be able to clearly articulate their goals, mutual responsibilities, and measures of success before embarking on such a relationship. We are often fuzzy about what we want from a partnership; the sides hope that goodwill and the desire for cooperation can carry the project through. All too frequently, entropy grabs hold of a project at this point, and the goodwill and motivation dissipate in the face of competing demands and time pressures. It is critical to be clear about the project goals, who is responsible for what activities, and how success is defined. Without satisfying these criteria, we may not be quite ready to declare a partnership.

Finally, it is important to anticipate the time commitment that a partnership requires. Real partnership is not episodic or short-lived; it takes time to develop, mature, and yield long-term benefits.

Leadership

The leaders needed in this environment are those willing to step outside the comfort zone of institutional norms and seek new relationships. They are more adept at building bridges than erecting walls. They also excel at communicating vision and strategy. Management deals mostly with the status quo; leadership deals mostly with change. Partnership requires genuine leadership.

Diana G. Oblinger is former vice president for information resources and CIO at the University of North Carolina system. She is currently senior fellow at the EDUCAUSE Center for Applied Research.

7

Leadership in a
Global Learning Marketspace

Two ponds of equal size stand at the foot of a mountain. Streams of a similar kind feed both ponds, the vitality of the melting snow flowing into them. But one is stagnant and plagued by algae; little life can be seen along its edges. The other is vibrant, bright, and blue; wildlife regularly visit its shores and partake of its water. What makes the difference is that the life-giving pond has an outlet.

There are many types of higher education institutions, with many types of leaders. For the purposes of this chapter, as with the ponds, we see mainly two. Both types may well be fed by similar streams of strategic planning guidelines, mission, and perhaps even values. However, in terms of the learning marketspace, the institution and leader that begin from a perspective of seeking outlets or partners will vitalize themselves through the process. Those who resist will become increasingly less relevant in an increasingly more global learning marketspace. Furthermore, a key criterion for being ready to partner in this marketspace is having competent leadership committed to the effort.

In this closing chapter, we identify and examine the fundamentals of the leadership that will be needed to partner in a learning marketspace, and examine the special challenges that arise in balancing the global with the parochial concerns of higher education institutions.

Leadership Fundamentals

In a *Fast Company* interview conducted by Polly LaBarre (2000), philosopher Peter Koestenbaum (the author of *Leadership: The Inner Side of Greatness*) asks people to "think of leadership as the sum of two vectors: competence (specialty, skills, know-how) and authenticity (identity, character, attitude)." He goes on to state that "the central leadership attribute is the ability to manage polarity" (p. 226).

Based on these three key areas, we have developed an LMS leadership model (summarized in Table 7.1) that examines the ways in which leaders might enhance their ability to foster partnerships in the learning marketspace:

- *Competence*. What are the important leadership skills and abilities in the learning marketspace?

- *Authenticity*. How do you identify leaders who are genuinely committed to LMS partnering?

- *Polarity*. What are the oppositional qualities, ideas, and systems that need to be balanced in the complex environments encountered in LMS partnering?

Competence

A key competency of LMS leaders is to have a deep understanding of the variety of higher education institutional roles and cultures, as the culture and makeup of an institution greatly influence its ability to be a successful LMS partner.

George Keller (1999–2000) identifies at least four distinct college and university cultures in the United States today: the research university; the small liberal arts college; the state colleges and universities, colleges of technology, and regional private colleges; and the two-year colleges, proprietary schools, and the less-well-endowed private colleges. For institutions in the first two cultural

Table 7.1. LMS Leadership Model

Competence	Authenticity	Polarity
Understands institutional cultures and effectively deals with cultural dissonance and technology backlash	Exhibits emotional intelligence and an internal locus of control	Sustains existing needed technologies while protecting and promoting disruptive technologies
Demonstrates technological literacy and uses technologies to communicate and increase his or her accessibility	Demonstrates values of collaboration, teamwork, and relationships by working with partners and developing leaders	Promotes co-opetition and actively seeks public and private partners among competitors
Functions effectively in a multilinear mode and within multiple partnerships, and is skilled at networking	Exhibits transformational leadership through commitment to information sharing and basing decisions on the greater good	Accelerates global thinking while supporting necessary and space-based strategies

types, any attempt at LMS partnering is likely to be met with resistance. Institutions that fall into the third and fourth types may be more receptive to LMS partnerships, especially community colleges that Keller describes as "remarkably open to planning for new forms of service, different kinds of faculty, and novel forms of academic delivery" (p. 3).

In *The Four Cultures of the Academy*, Bergquist (1992) elaborates on the cultural dynamics of higher education institutions, describing four primary cultures within them as managerial, developmental, negotiating, and collegial. Donald Hanna (2000) proposes an additional culture, the entrepreneurial, which "values the ability to change and to change quickly, to respond to market forces, to connect with and generate support from external audiences and constituencies, and to introduce new ideas, programs, delivery mechanisms, goals, and purposes" into the other, more internal, cultures. He adds, "It is no wonder that this [entrepreneurial] culture often generates significant political ill will internally, especially within the collegial culture, while at the same time deriving significant support from outside the university's other cultures" (p. 96).

For leaders to understand fully the magnitude of the challenge of operating within an LMS partnership, they must be prepared and able to deal with the internal responses toward the innovation within their specific type of institution and its corresponding culture. Essentially, those within the academy often perceive the entrepreneurial LMS as a counterculture compared to the age-old academic established and codified cultures. Part of this response is due to the massive and far-reaching dimensional changes that are affecting higher education through the emergence of a global learning marketspace.

Another requisite competency for LMS leaders is simply to communicate using the technologies that support the partnerships. Unfortunately, we know far too many higher education leaders who do not yet read and respond to their own e-mail. E-mail is the workhorse of the learning marketspace, of e-commerce, and of the Internet; you simply have to communicate by means of the technology to understand its implications.

It is ironic that many of today's leaders within higher education admit to technology illiteracy and then do little to correct the situation. Richard Varn (1999) insists this can no longer be tolerated: "Higher education should not be where we passionately and methodically search for new insight into how we learn, how to use technology, and the factors and methods of human organization and success, just so we may ignore such insights when it comes to our own programs. We must practice what we teach" (pp. 74–75). Hanna (2000) concurs: "Respected leaders today are excellent and broad communicators, which includes reading and answering unfiltered e-mail as a number one priority" (p. 172). In short, leaders who promote the concept of access in their learning marketspace cannot afford to remain inaccessible themselves.

LMS leaders no longer can plan on functioning in a unilinear mode; they must be able to envision, implement, and evaluate multiple partnerships at one time, realizing that they are unlikely to be able to anticipate marketspace competition on their own but they can probably do so through partnership. Thus they must be skilled at developing interdependencies and networks. Gary Neilson, Bruce Pasternack, and Albert Viscio (2000) propose that leaders in e-organizations must be able to create an environment in which others can succeed, to create the capacity for change as opposed to forcing change on others, and to manage partnerships with a "fair degree of independent control" rather than a command-and-control mentality. Likewise, Don Tapscott (1997) suggests that this approach to leadership is the antithesis of the old-style, brilliant-visionary, take-charge, rally-the-troops type.

You might assume that current job descriptions for executive positions in higher education would require these competencies. To confirm this assumption, we examined the descriptions of all of the open executive positions (academic vice presidents and provosts, executive directors, state commissioners and chancellors, university and college presidents, vice presidents and deputy directors, and executive positions in distance learning) listed in the *Chronicle of Higher Education* from three weeks chosen at random: February 25, April 7, and April 21, 2000. Varying with the specifics of the 127 executive position descriptions listed during these three weeks, the major themes were

- Managing and developing staff

- Overseeing fundraising, alumni relations, and donor relationships

- Leading public relations and marketing

- Overseeing campus functions and business operations

Most of these position descriptions maintained an internal focus—the campus—and promoting it to the community and sponsors. This was also true for most of the partnership skills that were required (such as collaborating with "constituencies"). Of the 127 descriptions, 21 (or roughly 16 percent) explicitly stated that they were looking for skills for partnering beyond their campus. For example, the Community College of Rhode Island requested that its president exhibit a "successful record of promoting partnerships and building coalitions with various groups such as higher education institutions, public schools, business and labor." Garden City Community College in Kansas requested a president who will "forge and maintain partnerships with business, industry, community organizations and educational institutions." The fact that many of the position descriptions that indicate the need for a leader with partnership skills were from community colleges is consistent with Keller's analysis that this type of institution is more open to novel alliances and forms of delivery than the others.

With the growth of the learning marketspace (see Chapter Two), institutions of all types should look for leaders with LMS competencies, especially those who understand and are willing to integrate different cultures, who communicate through the technologies that support the learning marketspace, and who are able to function in a multilinear mode, fostering partnerships and building networks. They will lead institutions into the future.

Authenticity

Given the essential competencies for LMS leadership, how do you identify whether a leader is "authentic," that is, genuinely committed to developing these competencies and partnering in an LMS? To check for such authenticity, you might look closely at how leaders work with others, and at the value they place on the resulting relationships.

According to Janet Poley (2000), "Leaders are considered to be 'moving with' others as they listen, empathize, bridge and network;

they are 'moving against' others as they lead using persuasion and bargaining." Academic leaders, she says, "need to learn more about the skills the business world calls emotional intelligence: the human capacities of empathy, self-awareness, and self-regulation, and the ability to reward and motivate oneself and others" (p. 174). Elaine Showalter (1999) quotes psychologist Daniel Goleman, author of *Emotional Intelligence* (1995), in her article about incivility in academe: "Emotional competence is particularly central to leadership, and for star performance, in all jobs, in every field, emotional competence is twice as important as cognitive abilities." She adds that executives understand "that emotional intelligence is not simply intuitive, and that it can be taught and learned" (p. B4).

In *The Leadership Engine*, Noel Tichy (1997) describes the fundamental nature of leaders of winning organizations, pointing out characteristics that resonate with emotional intelligence and that can be used to judge authenticity. Leaders, he says, take direct responsibility for the development of other leaders, have "teachable values," admit mistakes, and show their vulnerability.

The learning marketspace clearly requires leaders who both know themselves and also recognize and cultivate the tremendous power of collaboration and teamwork. Emotional intelligence brings a new capacity to LMS leadership. Knowing this, you can identify authenticity by determining if leaders visibly work to develop other leaders. Do they promote such development in people at all levels of their organization? Do they promote development of their counterparts in a partnering organization?

In addition, you can look for LMS leaders who function as transformers. *Transformational leadership* is a term coined by James McGregor Burns in his classic book *Leadership* (1978). He notes that most leaders and followers are *transactional*, that is, they approach followers to exchange one thing for another. Transactions make up the bulk of the relationships among leaders and followers, especially in groups such as a legislature or a higher education constituency.

Transformational leadership, however, is more complex and potent. Burns says the transformational leader looks for potential motives in followers, seeks to satisfy higher ends, and engages the full person of the follower. The result of such leadership is a relationship of mutual stimulation and elevation; transformational leaders view partnership as developing a relationship of mutual needs, aspirations, and values.

In short, you should look for leaders who exhibit this internal rather than external locus of control in both their own and others' personal and professional development. Transformational leaders in the learning marketspace have a sense that they can influence what happens in their LMS partnership, which they see as part of a larger and grander vision, attending to the social contract, meeting a larger societal need, and valuing relationships. This attendance to a grander vision includes a commitment to the value of information sharing to ensure that institutions—especially public higher education institutions—do not privatize knowledge that is essential to society. In an era of digital competition, the public is best served by information sharing, not resource hoarding; as Seth Shulman (1999) urges, "Whenever possible, vital intellectual resources must be shared so that they can benefit everyone, rather than enrich a select few. We must not allow the escalating privatization of knowledge to choke productivity, magnify social inequalities, and erode our democratic institutions" (p. A64).

Polarity

LMS leaders must allow and manage polarity, that is, pay attention simultaneously to what appear as opposites. Koestenbaum says that "managing polarity teaches us that there are no solutions—there are only changes of attitude. . . . The visionary leader thinks big, thinks new, thinks ahead" (LaBarre, 2000, pp. 228, 230). A change in attitude toward disruptive innovation—and toward the learning marketspace itself—begins with the leader.

LMS leaders especially must support and reward the development and implementation of disruptive technologies (see Chapter Six). As part of managing polarity in a world of ubiquitous connections, they must accelerate the transfer of place-based strategies, systems, and processes to virtual network spaces. In Kelly's terms, the LMS leader will more often choose "the more connected, the more open system, the more widely linked standard" (1998, p. 81).

There are many polarities that the LMS leader must understand, allow, and balance, among them the following:

- Public and private partnerships

- Higher education and business and industry

- Institutional needs and the needs of the individual learner

- Competition among partners and, at the same time, cooperation and collaboration (known as "co-opetition")

- Emerging fringe markets and the needs of the mainstream existing organization

- Reproducing existing structures (that is, sustaining technologies) and building new structures (disruptive technologies)

- The need for technology and the need for relationships

- Intellectual capital and social capital

- Global and parochial concerns

Despite the enormous need to manage such polarities, many higher education leaders resist managing them because the risks are also enormous. In *Leading Without Power* (1997), Max De Pree discusses the crux of the issue:

By avoiding risk we really risk what's most important in life—reaching toward growth, our potential, and a true contribution to a common good. Sometimes we risk the present, and we do so most often consciously. Most of the time we risk the future, and we do so unconsciously. Many times we think about risking only material things. But in subtle, unspoken collaboration, we often risk persons and their future and their potential. In fact the degree to which we are prepared to take risks determines the degree to which we as individuals and as organizations can reach our potential. [pp. 137–139]

Imagine that you are a leader at a prestigious liberal arts college and have been approached by representatives of Global Education Network with an invitation to contribute course material to a proposed for-profit Web site providing online liberal arts education for adults. The venture could earn your institution upwards of $2.5 million annually. Should your college attend to the fringe market or the mainstream? Or should it manage polarity and attend to both?

Imagine that you are Ihor Katernyak, director of the Technology Promotion Center at the Lviv Institute of Management in the Ukraine (www.lim.lviv.ua/english/de), working to establish a set of global business, industry, and educational partnerships to support the start of a virtual university for the Ukraine. Katernyak must overcome tremendous infrastructure barriers, but his personal commitment and courage—coupled with the enormous enthusiasm of the rank and file—makes for great potential. Should the Lviv Institute attend to the needs of the Ukraine as a whole for a learning infrastructure, or should it address the needs of the individual partners? Or might it manage polarity and do both?

Too many higher education institutions and too many of their leaders treat the learning marketspace as a technical challenge rather than embracing these polarities and developing authentic answers to basic questions about learning and leadership. To do so requires more than competence; it requires authenticity and, above all, the capacity to anticipate, absorb, and thrive in the realm of polarity.

In sum, there is clearly an interplay among the components of the LMS leadership model described here. The competencies interact with the way an individual leader builds upon his or her authenticity. This is where emotional intelligence is used to its best advantage in decision making and team enhancement. Likewise, there is interplay between the authenticity dimension and the polarity of the environment. This is exemplified in balancing high-tech and high-touch needs, the good of the individual and the good of society, and external versus internal locus of control.

Preparing for a Global Future

Perhaps the greatest leadership challenge of all is dealing with the tension between global and parochial concerns. Although we understand the importance of thinking globally, higher education still for the most part lives parochially.

In *The Lexus and the Olive Tree* (1999), Thomas Friedman proposes that globalization is not just a phenomenon, not just a passing trend; the international system has replaced the cold war system. Globalization is the integration of capital, technology, and information across national borders; it has created a single global market, and to some degree a global educational village.

Friedman's metaphorical comparison of the Lexus (globalization) and the olive tree (culture, geography, tradition, and community) captures the reality of partnering in the learning marketspace.

The olive tree is the current organizational structure of learning as we have known it for centuries. It has formed the basis for socialization and continuity; it has been a sustaining institution, carefully passing on training and education from generation to generation; and it has been geographically as place-bound as any olive tree. Public education has been locally funded and nourished through state appropriations and student tuition in order to meet the educational needs deemed important by state officials. The primary threat has been mainly from local or regional competition, which might take over the student enrollment, or from slow starvation of the public funds required to sustain the ongoing needs of the institution.

In applying Friedman's metaphor to education, the Lexus represents virtual universities, mega-universities, for-profit educational ventures, and the corporate and industrial enterprises demanding more than what public education has been able to deliver. Friedman says sustenance, improvement, prosperity, and modernization are the keys to understanding the Lexus in his economic analysis; it is characterized by the "anonymous, transitional, homogenizing, standardizing market forces and technologies that make up today's globalizing economic system" (1999, p. 29), forces that we believe also contribute to an increasingly global educational system.

Education seemed capable of keeping up in the agrarian times of the olive-tree era, and it even made the shift to the industrial age. But the digital age requires more responsiveness and more results-oriented products. Education fundamentally thrives on technological advances that form the cornerstone of the knowledge-based economy. In the Lexus model, educational providers are global in their appeal and delivery. Lexus players see tremendous need for education and training and identify the weaknesses of the place-bound olive tree (read: place-bound higher educational institutions). They form powerful strategic alliances with best-in-class content experts, technical teams, and delivery mechanisms. They place quality at the center of their enterprise, knowing that learners demand—indeed, have a world full of—educational options.

The learning marketspace is the stage on which the olive tree and the Lexus perform together. As we enter the first decade of the new century, can higher education as we have known it and the emerging learning marketspace coexist? We contend that they must, for education to continue to be a freeing, improving, shining light amid the darkness of ignorance. Together, they can enlighten all of humanity, if we can all agree on what must be done. The task is no longer geographically bound, or time-bound, or technology-bound. Yet, as with the backlash against globalization, so there exists a reaction to a globalized educational structure.

Leadership in the learning marketspace is not manifested in technology or techniques; it takes the true form of competent, authentic leaders capable of managing polarity. Moreover, it takes courage, and both institutional and personal commitment to partnering.

References

Bergquist, W. H. *The Four Cultures of the Academy.* San Francisco: Jossey-Bass, 1992.

Burns, J. M. *Leadership.* New York: HarperCollins, 1978.

De Pree, M. *Leading Without Power.* San Francisco: Jossey-Bass, 1997.

Friedman, T. L. *The Lexus and the Olive Tree.* New York: Farrar, Straus & Giroux, 1999.

Goleman, D. *Emotional Intelligence.* New York: Bantam, 1995.

Hanna, D. E. (ed.). *Higher Education in an Era of Digital Competition: Choices and Challenges.* Madison, Wis.: Atwood, 2000.

Keller, G. "The Emerging Third Stage in Higher Education Planning." *Planning for Higher Education,* Winter 1999–2000, pp. 1–7.

Kelly, K. *New Rules for the New Economy: 10 Radical Strategies for a Connected World.* New York: Penguin, 1998.

LaBarre, P. "Do You Have the Will to Lead?" [Interview with Peter Koestenbaum.] *Fast Company,* 2000, *32,* pp. 222–226. [www.fastcompany.com/online/32/koestenbaum.html].

Neilson, G. L., Pasternack, B., and Viscio, A. J. "Up the E-Organization! A Seven-Dimensional Model for the Centerless Enterprise." *Strategy and Business,* 2000, *18*(1), 52–61.

Poley, J. "Leadership in the Age of Knowledge." In D. Hanna (ed.), *Higher Education in an Era of Digital Competition: Choices and Challenges.* Madison, Wis.: Atwood, 2000.

Showalter, E. "Taming the Rampant Incivility in Academe." *The Chronicle of Higher Education,* Jan. 15, 1999, p. B4.

Shulman, S. "We Need Ways to Own and Share Knowledge." *The Chronicle of Higher Education,* Feb. 19, 1999, p. A64.

Tapscott, D. *The Digital Economy: Promise and Peril in the Age of Networked Intelligence.* New York: McGraw-Hill, 1997.

Tichy, N. *The Leadership Engine.* New York: HarperCollins, 1997.

Varn, R. J. "Higher Education: From Industrial Age to Information Age Education." *Converge*, Feb. 1999. [www.convergemag.com/Publications/CNVGFeb99/inforich/inforich.shtm].

Index